GoodFood
MAGAZINE

101 RECIPES FOR KIDS

D0928338

10 9 8 7 6 5 4 3 2 1

Published in 2008 by BBC Books,
an imprint of Ebury Publishing
A Random House Group Company

The Random House Group Limited
Reg. No. 954009

Addresses for companies within the Random House Group can be found at www.randomhouse.co.uk

A CIP catalogue record for this book is available from the British Library.

The Random House Group Limited supports The Forest Stewardship Council (FSC), the leading international forest certification organization. All our titles that are printed on Greenpeace approved FSC certified paper carry the FSC logo. Our paper procurement policy can be found at www.rbooks.co.uk/environment

To buy books by your favourite authors and register for offers visit www.rbooks.co.uk

Printed and bound by Firmengruppe APPL, aprinta druck, Wemding, Germany
Colour origination by Dot Gradations Ltd, UK

Commissioning Editor: Lorna Russell
Project Editor: Laura Higginson
Designer: Annette Peppis
Production: David Brimble
Picture Researchers: Gabby Harrington and Natalie Lief

ISBN: 9781846074240

GoodFood
MAGAZINE

101 RECIPES FOR KIDS
TRIED-AND-TESTED IDEAS

Editors
Angela Nilsen and Jeni Wright

Contents

Traditional porridge oats are best here, as jumbo or organic oats tend to give a more 'lacey', sugary finish.

Bumper Oat Cookies

175g/6oz butter, cut into pieces
175g/6oz demerara sugar
100g/4oz golden syrup
85g/3oz plain flour
½ tsp bicarbonate of soda
250g/9oz porridge oats
1 tsp ground cinnamon
100g/4oz dried apricots, chopped
75–80g pack dried sour cherries
100g/4oz stem ginger, chopped
2 tbsp boiling water
1 medium egg, beaten

Takes 45–50 minutes • Makes 18

1 Pre-heat the oven to 180°C/Gas 4/fan 160°C. Line several baking sheets with baking parchment. Warm the butter, sugar and golden syrup in a pan over a medium heat until the butter has melted. Stir in flour, bicarbonate of soda, oats, cinnamon, dried fruits and ginger, then water, and finally egg. Leave to cool.
2 With damp hands, shape the mixture into 18 balls then flatten them on to the baking sheets – allow plenty of space for spreading. Bake for 15–20 minutes until golden. (This will give a soft, chewy cookie. For a crisper one, reduce the heat to 160°C/Gas 3/fan 140°C, bake for an extra 5–10 minutes.)
3 Allow the cookies to cool on the trays briefly, then lift on to a cooling rack. The cookies will keep in an airtight container, separated by baking parchment, for up to 1 week.

• Per cookie 236 kcalories, protein 3g, carbohydrate 37g, fat 10g, saturated fat 5g, fibre 2g, sugar 13g, salt 0.3g

These light blueberry muffins have a fruity, juicy taste and are perfect for a snack, a lunchbox or a homecoming treat after school.

Berry Buttermilk Muffins

400g/14oz plain flour
175g/6oz golden caster sugar
1 tbsp baking powder
finely grated zest 1 lemon
½ tsp salt
284ml carton buttermilk
2 eggs, beaten
85g/3oz butter, melted
250g/9oz fresh blueberries

Takes about 40 minutes • Makes 12

1 Pre-heat the oven to 200°C/Gas 6/fan 180°C. Butter a 12-hole muffin tin.
In a large bowl, combine the flour, sugar, baking powder, lemon zest and salt. In a separate bowl, mix together the buttermilk, eggs and butter.
2 Make a well in the centre of the dry ingredients and pour in the buttermilk mixture. Stir until the ingredients are just combined and the mixture is quite stiff, but don't overmix. Lightly fold in the berries, then spoon the mixture into the tins to fill generously.
3 Bake for about 25 minutes until risen and pale golden on top. Leave to cool in the tins for about 5 minutes before turning out gently on to a wire rack, as the muffins are quite delicate when hot.

• Per muffin 253 kcalories, protein 5g, carbohydrate 44g, fat 7g, saturated fat 4g, fibre 1g, sugar 15g, salt 0.91g

These healthy and tasty bars are just the thing for a hungry mob
to snack on when they are after something sweet.

Muesli Fruit-and-Nut Bars

100g/4oz butter, plus extra for the tin
100g/4oz light muscovado sugar
4 tbsp golden syrup
100g pack pecan nuts
300g/12oz unsweetened muesli,
preferably organic
1 medium ripe banana, mashed

Takes 30–40 minutes • Makes 12

1 Pre-heat the oven to 180°C/Gas 4/fan 160°C. Butter and base-line an 18x28cm/7x11in or 22cm/8½in square tin with baking parchment. Melt the butter, sugar and syrup in a medium pan on a low heat, stirring until sugar has dissolved. Cool slightly.
2 Chop half the nuts. Stir the muesli, banana and the chopped nuts into the pan until well coated. Spoon the mixture into the tin and press down with the back of a spoon until firmly packed.
3 Scatter the whole nuts over, pressing them lightly into mixture. Bake for 20–25 minutes until dark golden and the edges start to crisp. Leave in the tin until cold, then loosen edges with a knife. Cut into slices. Will keep in an airtight container for up to 5 days.

• Per bar 330 kcalories, protein 5g, carbohydrate 34g, fat 20g, saturated fat 5g, fibre 3g, sugar 12g, salt 0.24g

If you want to encourage your children to learn how to bake, this is a great recipe to start them off.

Simple Jammy Biscuits

200g/8oz self-raising flour
100g/4oz golden caster sugar
100g/4oz butter
1 egg, lightly beaten
4 tbsp strawberry jam

Takes about 25 minutes • Makes 12

1 Pre-heat the oven to 190°C/Gas 5/fan 170°C. Rub the flour, sugar and butter together until the mixture resembles breadcrumbs. Alternatively, you can do this in the food processor. Next, add enough egg to bring the mixture together to form a stiff dough.

2 Flour your hands and shape the dough into a tube, about 5cm/2in in diameter. Cut into 2cm/¾in thick slices and place on a large baking sheet. Space the slices so they are well apart, as the mixture will spread when baking.

3 Make a small indentation in the middle of each slice with the end of a wooden spoon, and drop a teaspoon of jam in the centre. Bake for 10–15 minutes until slightly risen and just golden. Cool on a wire rack.

• Per biscuit 170 kcalories, protein 2g, carbohydrate 25g, fat 8g, saturated fat 5g, fibre 0.5g, sugar 13g, salt 0.3g

Introduction

Many of us at *Good Food Magazine* are working mums and dads, so we know what it's like to have to provide delicious, nutritious meals for children or the whole family each and every busy day.

So this is where this collection of 101 recipes can help. This book brings together some of the very best recipes we've ever published for kids, so you'll never be stuck for ideas when your children say, 'We're starving, what can we eat?' Whether it's a filling but nutritious packed lunch, a quick and easy snack for hungry, homecoming schoolchildren, or a supper you can all share sat round the table, we've got suggestions for all of these occasions and more. Not forgetting some exciting party ideas and special sweet treats for when they've been good!

Many of these recipes can be made by the children themselves, with or without a little adult help, and they've all been tried and tested on kids, so we know they'll become firm favourites. Providing a healthy diet for children is very important, which is why you'll find a nutritional breakdown with every recipe so you know exactly what they are eating.

Turn the pages now and see what's in store. We know you and your kids will be inspired to get cooking straight away.

Angela Nilsen and Jeni Wright
BBC Good Food Magazine

Notes and Conversion tables

NOTES ON THE RECIPES
• Eggs are large in the UK and Australia unless stated otherwise.
• Wash all fresh produce before preparation.
• Recipes contain nutritional analyses for 'sugar', which means the total sugar content including all natural sugars in the ingredients unless otherwise stated.

OVEN TEMPERATURES

Gas	°C	Fan °C	°F	Oven temp.
¼	110	90	225	Very cool
½	120	100	250	Very cool
1	140	120	275	Cool or slow
2	150	130	300	Cool or slow
3	160	140	325	Warm
4	180	160	350	Moderate
5	190	170	375	Moderately hot
6	200	180	400	Fairly hot
7	220	200	425	Hot
8	230	210	450	Very hot
9	240	220	475	Very hot

APPROXIMATE WEIGHT CONVERSIONS
• All the recipes in this book list both imperial and metric measurements. Conversions are approximate and have been rounded up or down. Follow one set of measurements only; do not mix the two.
• Cup measurements, which are used by cooks in Australia and America, have not been listed here as they vary from ingredient to ingredient. Please use kitchen scales to measure dry/solid ingredients.

SPOON MEASURES

Spoon measurements are level unless otherwise specified.

- 1 teaspoon = 5ml
- 1 tablespoon = 15ml
- 1 Australian tablespoon = 20ml (cooks in Australia should measure 3 teaspoons where 1 tablespoon is specified in a recipe)

APPROXIMATE LIQUID CONVERSIONS

metric	imperial	AUS	US
50ml	2fl oz	¼ cup	¼ cup
125ml	4fl oz	½ cup	½ cup
175ml	6fl oz	¾ cup	¾ cup
225ml	8fl oz	1 cup	1 cup
300ml	10fl oz/½ pint	½ pint	1¼ cups
450ml	16fl oz	2 cups	2 cups/1 pint
600ml	20fl oz/1 pint	1 pint	2½ cups
1 litre	35fl oz/1¾ pints	1¾ pints	1 quart

If you use chickpeas instead of beans, this will make a simple, but very tasty, houmous.

Beany Pitta Pockets

400g can white beans (such as cannellini or haricot), drained and rinsed
1 garlic clove, peeled and roughly chopped
2 tbsp olive oil
juice ½ lemon, or more, to taste
4 wholemeal pitta breads
½ cucumber, cut into sticks
4 small tomatoes

Takes 15 minutes • Makes 4

1 Purée the beans in a blender or food processor with the garlic, oil, juice of half a lemon and seasoning. Taste and add more lemon juice and seasoning, if you like. If the purée tastes good but is too stiff, slacken it with a drop or two of hot water from the kettle.
2 Warm the pittas in the toaster, then cut off one end of each and open out the pockets.
3 Stuff the pittas with the bean purée, cucumber and tomatoes. Wrap and pack into airtight containers.

• Per pitta pocket 265 kcalories, protein 11.4g, carbohydrate 41g, fat 7.4g, saturated fat 1.1g, fibre 7.3g, sugar 5.6, salt 1.37g

These make perfectly proportioned sandwiches for kids, and grown-ups like them too.

Mini Chicken Sandwiches

100g/4oz cooked chicken, shredded
1 carrot, grated
½ red pepper, seeded and finely chopped
2 heaped tbsp sweetcorn kernels (canned or cooked from frozen)
1 tbsp mayonnaise, or more to taste
squeeze of fresh lemon juice
knob of soft butter
4 slices wholemeal or granary bread

Takes 15 minutes • Makes 8

1 Mix the chicken in a bowl with the carrot, red pepper and sweetcorn. Add one tablespoon of mayonnaise, a squeeze of lemon juice, and some seasoning. Stir well to mix, then taste and add more mayonnaise and seasoning, if you like.
2 Butter the bread and make two sandwiches with the filling.
3 Cut each sandwich into quarters. Wrap and pack into airtight containers.

• Per sandwich 98 kcalories, protein 5.1g, carbohydrate 10.6g, fat 4.2g, saturated fat 1.5g, fibre 1.4g, sugar 2.5g, salt 0.31g

Packed with slow-releasing carbohydrates, this salad makes a tasty change from sandwiches and combines two kids' favourites: sausages and pasta.

Sausage Pasta Salad

2 chipolata sausages
85g/3oz dried fusilli or other short pasta shape
2 tsp olive oil
2 cherry tomatoes, cut into wedges
2 spring onions, finely chopped
2 tbsp home-made or ready-made tomato salsa

Takes 25 minutes, plus cooling • Serves 2

1 Heat the grill to high and grill the sausages for about 15 minutes or until cooked through, turning them occasionally. Leave to cool then slice into bite-sized pieces.
2 Cook the pasta in a pan of salted boiling water for 8–10 minutes, or according to the packet instructions, until tender. Drain into a sieve and hold under the cold tap until cool.
3 Shake the pasta well to remove excess water, then tip into a bowl and stir in the oil to prevent the shapes sticking together. Mix in the sausages, tomatoes, onions and salsa. Taste for seasoning, then divide between two airtight containers.

• Per portion 244 kcalories, protein 8.6g, carbohydrate 36.1g, fat 8.3g, saturated fat 2.3g, fibre 1.8g, sugar 2.4g, salt 0.95g

This tart is well worth making to use in several packed lunches because it keeps in the fridge for 3 days. Using ready-made pastry saves on preparation time.

Pea and Ham Tart

250g/9oz ready-made shortcrust pastry
250g/9oz frozen peas, thawed
4 eggs
200ml carton crème fraîche
85g/3oz mature Cheddar, grated
85g/3oz thickly sliced ham, cut into chunks

Takes 55 minutes, plus thawing time • Cuts into 6 slices

1 Pre-heat the oven to 200°C/Gas 6/fan 180°C. Roll out the pastry on a floured surface and use to line a deep 20–22cm/8–8½in flan tin. Lightly prick the pastry base with a fork, fill with crumpled foil and bake blind for 15 minutes.

2 Meanwhile, whiz the peas, eggs and crème fraîche in a food processor with salt and pepper until just blended; stir in the cheese and ham.

3 Remove the foil from the pastry and lower the oven temperature to 180°C/Gas 4/fan 160°C. Pour the filling into the pastry case and bake for 35 minutes or until the filling is golden and just set. Leave to cool in the tin, then remove and cut into six slices. Wrap and pack into airtight containers.

• Per slice 437 kcalories, protein 16g, carbohydrate 24g, fat 31g, saturated fat 16g, fibre 3g, added sugar none, salt 1.05g

Older children can pop these in the oven themselves. They're great for any child on the move, but if you're heading out with them in the car, don't forget paper napkins to cut down on mess.

Ham and Pepper Wraps

4 soft flour or corn tortilla wraps
8 small or 4 large slices ham
2 roasted peppers from a jar, well drained and roughly chopped
handful of Cheddar, grated

Takes 15–20 minutes • Makes 4

1 Pre-heat the oven to 180°C/Gas 4/fan 160°C. Lay the tortillas on a flat surface and place one or two slices of ham over each one. Sprinkle the peppers and cheese over the ham, leaving a 2cm/¾in edge at one end. Starting at the other end, roll the tortillas up as tightly as you can. Wrap each tortilla in foil and twist the ends to seal.

2 Place the wraps directly on the oven shelf and cook for 15 minutes or until the cheese starts to melt.

3 To eat, peel off the foil and wrap each tortilla in a paper napkin.

• Per wrap 175 kcalories, protein 10g, carbohydrate 17g, fat 8g, saturated fat 3g, fibre 2g, sugar 2g, salt 1.64g

A tasty packed lunch that contains protein to help build strong bones. To satisfy a hungry appetite, add a piece of fruit, some raw veg, a wedge of carrot cake and a drink to the lunchbox.

Easy Cheesey Tuna Bagel

1 bagel
50g/2oz full fat soft cheese with chives
½ x 100g can tuna in spring water or brine
4–5 cucumber slices

Takes 10 minutes • Serves 1

1 Split the bagel and spread both cut sides with the cheese and chives.
2 Drain and flake the tuna.
3 Sandwich the bagel halves together with the tuna and cucumber slices in between. Wrap in greaseproof paper or foil.

• Per bagel 344 kcalories, protein 18.5g, carbohydrate 31.6g, fat 16.9g, saturated fat 10.1g, fibre 1.7g, sugar 2.4g, salt 1.65g

This is a great break-time snack with a Mexican twist. Make it a healthier choice by including some crunchy lettuce leaves as well as some celery sticks to dunk.

Cool Lime Dip with Veg and Chips

2 celery sticks
1 carrot
¼ cucumber
large handful of tortilla chips (plain, spicy or blue corn)
salad leaves (optional)

—

FOR THE DIP
½ x 142ml carton soured cream or natural full fat yoghurt
handful of fresh coriander leaves, chopped
squeeze of fresh lime juice

Takes 10 minutes • Serves 1

1 Make the dip. Mix the soured cream or yoghurt with the coriander then squeeze in some lime juice to taste and season with a little salt and pepper.
2 Remove any strings from the celery then cut each stick in half. Peel the carrot and cut lengthways into sticks. Cut the cucumber lengthways into sticks.
3 Pack the dip in a small pot and seal the top, then pack into an airtight container with the veg and chips and some salad leaves, if you like.

• Per portion 287 kcalories, protein 8.8g, carbohydrate 38.9g, fat 11.7g, saturated fat 1.4g, fibre 6g, sugar 14.8g, salt 1.21g

A healthy lunch that's high in vitamin C, this colourful rice salad is a good way of getting lots of veggies and seeds into a child's diet.

Rainbow Rice

100g/4oz basmati, long grain or brown rice
1 small red pepper, seeded and finely chopped
½ cucumber, seeded and finely chopped
1 large carrot, grated
6 dried apricots, chopped
2 tbsp toasted pumpkin or sunflower seeds
2 tbsp olive oil
juice ½ orange

Takes 30 minutes • Serves 2 big kids or 4 small

1 Cook the rice according to the packet instructions. Drain, rinse and drain again.
2 Tip the rice into a large bowl and add all the other ingredients. Mix well and season to taste, then divide between airtight containers.

• Per portion (based on two servings) 225 kcalories, protein 5g, carbohydrate 32g, fat 14.5g, saturated fat 1.5g, fibre 3g, added sugar none, salt 0.035g

This is a healthy sandwich that's ideal for vegetarians. Simply double or triple the ingredients if you want to make more than one.

Apple Slaw Cheese Sarnie

1 rounded tbsp mayonnaise
squeeze of fresh lemon juice
small handful of grated Cheddar
or your kid's favourite hard cheese
1 dessert apple wedge, skin on,
coarsely grated
1 slim spring onion, finely chopped
2 slices wholemeal or granary bread

Takes 10 minutes • Makes 1

1 Mix the mayonnaise and lemon juice in a small bowl.
2 Stir in the grated cheese and apple and the chopped spring onion.
3 Spread the filling on one of the slices of bread and sandwich together with the other slice. Cut into four triangles. Pack in an airtight container.

• Per sarnie 467 kcalories, protein 12.6g, carbohydrate 44.3g, fat 27.8g, saturated fat 7.8g, fibre 5.8g, sugar 16.8g, salt 1.38g

This is a good way to introduce wholemeal flour into your family baking and makes a low-fat lunchbox treat.

Cheese and Marmite Scones

140g/5oz self-raising flour
140g/5oz wholemeal flour
1 tsp baking powder
50g/2oz cold butter, cut into small cubes
85g/3oz mature Cheddar, grated
1 egg
1 tbsp Marmite
2 tbsp Greek or other thick, natural yoghurt
3 tbsp milk, plus extra to glaze

Takes 25–35 minutes • Makes 8

1 Pre-heat the oven to 190°C/Gas 5/fan 170°C. Sift the flours and baking powder into a bowl. Rub in the butter with your fingertips until the mixture resembles fine breadcrumbs. Stir in half the cheese and make a well in the centre.

2 Whisk the egg in a jug with the Marmite, yoghurt and milk. Pour this mix into the well in the flour, and bring together with a knife to make a soft, but not sticky, dough. Add a little more milk if the dough is too dry.

3 Turn the dough on to a floured surface and roll out until 2cm/¾in thick. Stamp out four scones using a round cutter. Gather the trimmings to make another four scones. Put on a baking sheet, brush with milk and scatter over the remaining cheese. Bake for 10–12 minutes until golden. Cool on a wire rack.

• Per scone 226 kcalories, protein 9g, carbohydrate 25g, fat 11g, saturated fat 6g, fibre 2g, sugar 1g, salt 0.9g

Older children will enjoy the tanginess of the mustard, but you can leave it out if your child doesn't like it.

Special Beans on Toast

150g can baked beans
1 thick slice white bread
1 tsp grainy or other mustard
knob of soft butter
1 tbsp crème fraîche
large handful of grated Cheddar

Takes 10 minutes • Serves 1

1 Heat up the beans and toast the bread.
2 Stir the mustard into the beans and butter the toast.
3 Pile the beans on the toast and spoon the crème fraîche on top. Sprinkle over the cheese and grind over some pepper, if you like.

• Per serving 476 kcalories, protein 21.2g, carbohydrate 45.3g, fat 24.6g, saturated fat 14.5g, fibre 6.5g, sugar 10.6g, salt 3.51g

These cheesey nachos are great for nibbling on. The salsa can also be used as a healthy dip for another lunch or snack, served with vegetable sticks.

Sweetcorn and Tomato Nachos

1 avocado
198g can sweetcorn, drained
200g can chopped tomatoes
½ onion, peeled and finely chopped
large handful of fresh coriander
leaves, chopped
100g bag lightly salted tortilla chips
large handful of grated Cheddar

Takes 15 minutes • Serves 4

1 Halve the avocado and scoop out the stone. Make diagonal cuts in the flesh of each half, then repeat the cuts in the opposite direction so you have a criss-cross effect. Run a spoon inside the skin to release the avocado chunks.
2 Heat the grill to high. Make a salsa by mixing the avocado with the sweetcorn, tomatoes and their juice, onion and coriander.
3 Arrange the tortilla chips on a baking sheet. Spoon a little salsa on to each chip, then sprinkle all over with cheese. Grill for 3–5 minutes or until the cheese is bubbling and melted.

• Per portion 301 kcalories, protein 8.4g, carbohydrate 29g, fat 17.6g, saturated fat 4.1g, fibre 3.8g, sugar 6.4g, salt 1.21g

A warming and healthy snack that's quick to prepare, making it a real favourite among children and parents alike.

Seeded Bagel Tuna Melt

4 mixed seed bagels
200g can tuna in spring water, drained
1 tbsp mayonnaise
juice 1 lemon
1 bunch spring onions, roughly chopped
2 tomatoes, sliced
handful of grated mature Cheddar

Takes 10 minutes • Serves 4

1 Heat the grill to high. Split open the bagels, lay them on a baking sheet and toast both sides until golden.
2 Meanwhile, tip the tuna into a bowl and add the mayonnaise, lemon juice and spring onions. Season to taste and mix well.
3 Spread the tuna mix over the bottom half of each bagel and top with the tomato slices. Sprinkle over the grated cheese, then grill for 1 minute or until melted. Finish with the bagel tops and serve.

• Per bagel 257 kcalories, protein 17g, carbohydrate 29g, fat 9g, saturated fat 3g, fibre 2g, sugar 4g, salt 1.28g

Falafels are cheap and easy to make and the chickpeas from which they are made are a great source of folic acid and iron.

Spicy Falafels

2 tbsp sunflower or vegetable oil
1 small onion, peeled and finely chopped
1 garlic clove, peeled and crushed
400g can chickpeas, drained and rinsed
1 tsp ground cumin
1 tsp ground coriander (or use more cumin)
handful of flatleaf parsley, chopped, or 1 tsp dried mixed herbs
1 egg, beaten
pitta breads and salad, to serve

Takes 20 minutes • Makes 6

1 Heat one tablespoon of the oil in a large pan and fry the onion and garlic over a low heat for 5 minutes until softened. Tip into a large bowl with the chickpeas and ground spices, then mash together with a fork or potato masher until the chickpeas are totally broken down.

2 Stir the parsley or dried herbs into the chickpea mash with the egg and seasoning to taste. Squeeze the mixture together with your hands, mould into six balls and flatten into patties.

3 Heat the remaining oil in the pan, and fry the falafels over a medium heat for 3 minutes on each side, or until golden brown and firm. Serve hot or cold, stuffed into pitta breads with salad.

• Per falafel 105 kcalories, protein 5g, carbohydrate 8g, fat 6g, saturated fat 1g, fibre 2g, sugar 1g, salt 0.27g

A child-friendly version of the classic French snack.

Quick Croque-monsieur

2 slices wholemeal bread
1 egg
large handful of grated Cheddar
2 slices ham, cut into strips
pinch of English mustard powder

Takes 10 minutes • Serves 2

1 Heat the grill to high and toast the bread lightly on both sides.
2 While the bread is toasting, beat the egg in a bowl and mix in the cheese, ham and mustard.
3 Press the mixture on to one side of each piece of toast, then grill for 3–4 minutes or until golden and bubbling. Cut into halves to serve.

• Per serving 263 kcalories, protein 19g, carbohydrate 15g, fat 15g, saturated fat 7g, fibre 2g, added sugar none, salt 1.59g

This hearty, hot snack is the perfect mealtime solution for busy mums, taking no more than 20 minutes to prepare and even less time to eat!

Mexican Tortilla Triangles

2 tsp olive oil
2 soft flour or corn tortillas
85g/3oz Red Leicester, grated
100g/4oz cooked chicken, chopped
1 ripe tomato, sliced

Takes 15–20 minutes • Makes 8

1 Heat a non-stick frying pan over a medium heat, swirl one teaspoon of the oil around, then add a tortilla. Sprinkle a handful of the cheese over one half of the tortilla, followed by some chicken and a few tomato slices. Season with a little salt and pepper.
2 Cook for a few moments to melt the cheese, then fold over and cook until the tortilla is crisp.
3 Turn the tortilla out of the pan and cut into quarters. Repeat with the other tortilla and the remaining ingredients.

• Per triangle 104 kcalories, protein 7g, carbohydrate 6g, fat 6g, saturated fat 2.8g, fibre 0.3g, sugar 0.6g, salt 0.46g

These can be whipped up in minutes and kids will love to help you make them. Any leftover cakes can be put in the fridge and reheated the next day.

Cheesey Corn Cakes

175g/6oz self-raising flour
1 tsp baking powder
2 eggs
125ml/4fl oz milk
198g can sweetcorn, drained
100g/4oz mature Cheddar, grated
2 tbsp chopped chives
2 tsp sunflower oil

FOR THE DIP
2 ripe tomatoes, finely chopped
2 tbsp tomato ketchup

Takes 10–15 minutes • Makes 12

1 Make the dip by mixing the tomatoes and ketchup in a bowl. Set aside.
2 In another bowl, whisk the flour, baking powder, eggs and milk until smooth. Stir in the sweetcorn, cheese and chives. Season well.
3 Heat half the oil in a non-stick frying pan. Add six spoonfuls of the mixture to the pan and flatten out slightly with the back of the spoon, keeping them separate. Cook over a medium heat for 1½ minutes or until golden. Turn and cook on the other side, then remove from the pan and keep warm while you make six more cakes with the remaining oil and mixture. Serve with the dip.

• Per cake 127 kcalories, protein 5.4g, carbohydrate 16g, fat 4.8g, saturated fat 2.3g, fibre 0.8g, sugar 0.9g, salt 0.64g

These colourful, vegetarian Mexican wraps are quick and easy to prepare and great fun. Simply double the quantities if you've more than four mouths to feed.

Chilli Bean Wraps

1 onion, peeled and chopped
1 red pepper, seeded and chopped
1 garlic clove, chopped
2 tbsp vegetable oil
1 tsp mild chilli powder or ½ tsp hot
400g can baked beans
squeeze of fresh lime juice (optional)
4 soft flour or corn tortillas

Takes 10–15 minutes • Makes 4

1 Fry the onion, pepper and garlic in the oil until soft. Sprinkle over the chilli powder and cook for 1 minute, then add the baked beans and heat through.
2 Meanwhile, warm the tortillas according to the packet instructions.
3 Season the beans and add lime juice, if you like, then serve with the tortillas for all the family to assemble themselves.

• Per portion 284 kcalories, protein 10g, carbohydrate 43.4g, fat 9.1g, saturated fat 1.2g, fibre 5.7g, sugar 10.8g, salt 2.43g

This are fun eaten out of paper cones, and they are also a good side dish to accompany burgers, sausages or fish.

Sweet Potato Chips

4 sweet potatoes, scrubbed and cut lengthways into large chips
2 tbsp olive oil
2 tbsp light soy sauce
grated fresh nutmeg (optional)

Takes 40–50 minutes • Serves 4

1 Pre-heat the oven to 200°C/Gas 6/fan 180°C.
2 In a large bowl, toss the sweet potato chips with the oil and soy sauce.
3 Transfer the chips to a shallow roasting tin. Sprinkle with black pepper and nutmeg, if you like. Bake for 30–40 minutes, or until crisp.

• Per serving 207 kcalories, protein 3g, carbohydrate 38g, fat 6g, saturated fat 1g, fibre 4g, sugar 11g, salt 2g

A mouth-watering, hearty and warming snack that is also great for a family weekend brunch.

Ham and Eggy Bread

butter, for spreading and frying
2 thick slices bread
1 slice lean ham
1 egg
2 tbsp milk
1 tsp olive oil
home-made or ready-made tomato salsa, to serve

Takes 10 minutes • Serves 1

1 Lightly butter the slices of bread, then sandwich them together with the ham in between. Cut the sandwich diagonally in half.
2 In a shallow bowl, beat the egg and milk with seasoning to taste. Heat the oil with a small knob of butter in a non-stick frying pan until the butter foams. Dip the sandwich halves into the egg on both sides, then place in the pan.
3 Cook the sandwiches over a medium heat for 2 minutes on each side or until set and golden. Serve with spoonfuls of tomato salsa.

• Per serving 498 kcalories, protein 26g, carbohydrate 41g, fat 26g, saturated fat 12g, fibre 1g, sugar 4g, salt 3.10g

A healthy version of every student's favourite dish, these noodles take only a few minutes longer to prepare than the microwave version.

Home-made Pot Noodles

2 tsp Thai curry paste
3 spring onions, chopped
1 large carrot, grated
mugful of hot vegetable or chicken stock
handful of frozen peas
150g sachet straight-to-wok noodles
sesame seeds, to finish (optional)

Takes 10 minutes • Serves 1

1 Fry the curry paste in a pan over a medium heat for 2 minutes. Stir in the spring onions and carrot, then cook for 1 minute.
2 Pour in the stock and add the peas. Bring to the boil and simmer for 2 minutes or until the carrot is just cooked. Stir in the noodles and heat through.
3 Ladle into a mug or bowl and scatter with sesame seeds, if you like. Serve hot.

• Per serving 366 kcalories, protein 13g, carbohydrate 61g, fat 9g, saturated fat 1g, fibre 9g, sugar 14g, salt 2.85g

These spicy tortillas hit the spot after school, and they're so easy that you can let the children prepare them.

Mexican Bean Wraps

400g can mixed beans in chilli sauce
handful of cherry tomatoes, roughly chopped
4 soft flour or corn tortillas
2 handfuls of grated mature Cheddar
home-made or ready-made guacamole, to serve

Takes 15 minutes • Serves 2

1 Heat the grill to high. Tip the beans into a pan, stir in the tomatoes and cook over a medium heat for 5 minutes.
2 Divide the bean mixture among the tortillas, sprinkle a small handful of cheese over each, keeping a little in reserve, then roll up.
3 Put the wraps on a baking sheet and scatter over the remaining cheese. Grill for 2–3 minutes or until the cheese is golden and bubbling. Serve with guacamole.

• Per wrap 509 kcalories, protein 24g, carbohydrate 89g, fat 9g, saturated fat 5g, fibre 10g, sugar 5g, salt 2.41g

A mini version of the Hawaiian pizza, this speedy snack takes only minutes to prepare.

Ham and Pineapple Melts

1 wholemeal muffin
2 slices ham
2 pineapple rings, drained of juice
handful of grated mature Cheddar
Worcestershire sauce or tomato ketchup, to serve

Takes 10 minutes • Serves 1

1 Heat the grill to medium. Split the muffin in half, then toast lightly. Top each half with a slice of ham and a pineapple ring, then half the cheese.
2 Place on a baking sheet and grill for 3–4 minutes or until bubbling and golden. Serve with Worcestershire sauce or ketchup.

• Per serving 284 kcalories, protein 17g, carbohydrate 36g, fat 9g, saturated fat 5g, fibre none, sugar 6g, salt 2.21g

Make these with the kids for some after-school fun and some deliciously crumbly cookies to show for it.

Ginger Choc-chip Cookies

85g/3oz light muscovado sugar
200g/8oz butter, softened, plus extra for greasing
250g/9oz self-raising flour
2 tbsp golden syrup
1 tsp vanilla extract
100g/4oz plain chocolate drops or a bar plain chocolate, chopped
50g/2oz preserved ginger from a jar or crystallized ginger, roughly chopped

Takes 25 minutes, plus optional chilling
Makes 20

1 Pre-heat the oven to 200°C/Gas 6/fan 180°C. Butter and line two large baking sheets with non-stick baking parchment. Beat the sugar and butter together until light and creamy. Stir in the remaining ingredients until you have a soft dough.

2 Roll the dough into walnut-sized pieces and space out generously on the lined baking sheets. If you have time, chill in the fridge for 30 minutes.

3 Bake the cookies for 12–15 minutes or until lightly golden; they will still feel quite soft in the middle. Leave on the baking sheets until firm, about 5 minutes, then transfer to a wire rack to cool completely.

• Per cookie 169 kcalories, protein 1g, carbohydrate 20g, fat 10g, saturated fat 6g, fibre 1g, sugar 11g, salt 0.28g

The dough for these crisp and crunchy biscuits will keep for up to 3 months in the freezer and can be quickly baked as a pick-me-up after a long day at school.

Freezer Biscuits

250g pack butter, softened
200g/8oz muscovado sugar
2 eggs, beaten
1 tsp vanilla extract
200g/8oz self-raising flour
140g/5oz rolled oats
50g/2oz raisins or mixed dried fruit

OPTIONAL EXTRAS
50g/2oz chopped nuts
50g/2oz desiccated coconut

Takes 30 minutes • Makes 30

1 Cream the butter and sugar with an electric whisk until light and fluffy. Beat in the eggs and vanilla, then stir in the flour, oats and fruit, plus the nuts and coconut, if you like.
2 Spread half the mixture, in a line, down the centre of a large sheet of greaseproof paper. Pull over one edge of the paper and roll it round the mixture to make a tight sausage. Twist the ends of the paper and place in the freezer. Repeat with the other half.
3 To cook, pre-heat the oven to 180°C/Gas 4/fan 160°C. Unwrap a frozen sausage and cut off as many 5mm/¼in-thick discs as you need, using a sharp knife dipped in hot water. Place the discs on a baking sheet, spacing them apart to allow for spreading, then bake for 15 minutes or until golden brown. Cool for at least 5 minutes before eating.

• Per biscuit (without nuts and coconut) 138 kcalories, protein 2g, carbohydrate 16g, fat 8g, saturated fat 5g, fibre 1g, sugar 8g, salt 0.21g

This is a vegetarian version of the classic spaghetti Bolognese. Packed with iron and full of tasty veg, it makes an easy, nutritious supper.

Veggie Spag Bol

1 onion, peeled
1 carrot
1 celery stick
1 red pepper, halved and seeded
2 tbsp olive oil
100g/4oz red lentils
400g can tomatoes
600ml/1 pint vegetable stock
2 tsp dried oregano
½ tsp ground cinnamon
350g/12oz spaghetti
freshly grated, vegetarian,
Parmesan-style cheese, to serve

Takes 35–45 minutes • Serves 4
(easily halved)

1 Roughly chop the vegetables then whiz them in a food processor until finely chopped.
2 Heat the oil in a large pan and fry the vegetables for about 8 minutes until soft. Stir in the lentils, tomatoes, stock, oregano and cinnamon. Bring to the boil and season to taste, then reduce the heat, cover and simmer for 20 minutes.
3 Meanwhile, cook the spaghetti in a large pan of salted boiling water for 10–12 minutes, or according to the packet instructions, until tender. Drain well and serve with the sauce and grated cheese.

• Per serving 484 kcalories, protein 19g, carbohydrate 90g, fat 8g, saturated fat 1g, fibre 6g, added sugar none, salt 0.66g

Finger-shaped carrot pieces are fun and colourful in this pie but you could equally well use broccoli florets or wilted spinach.

Fish and Finger Pie

500g/1lb 2oz skinless cod fillet, cut into finger-length strips
2 large carrots, peeled and cut into finger-length strips
100g/4oz frozen peas
400g/14oz cooked peeled large prawns, thawed if frozen

FOR THE SAUCE
50g/2oz butter
50g/2oz plain flour
450ml/¾ pint milk
20g pack fresh parsley, leaves chopped
1 bay leaf

FOR THE TOPPING
200g/8oz plain flour
50g/2oz porridge oats
100g/4oz cold butter, diced
50g/2oz hard cheese, grated

Takes 1 hour • Serves 6 (easily halved)

1 Pre-heat the oven to 200°C/Gas 6/fan 180°C. Put the cod and carrots in a buttered baking dish. Sprinkle over peas and prawns.
2 Make the sauce. Melt the butter in a pan over a medium heat, add the flour and stir to form a smooth paste. Cook, stirring, for 2 minutes, then add the milk a little at a time, whisking vigorously until smooth. Bring to the boil, turn down the heat and simmer for 2 minutes. Remove from the heat and add the parsley, bay leaf and pepper to taste. Pour the sauce over the fish and vegetables.
3 Make the topping. Mix the flour and oats in a bowl, then mash in the butter with a fork until the mixture looks like large breadcrumbs. Stir in the cheese, then sprinkle over the sauce. Bake for 20–25 minutes or until the topping is golden and crunchy.

• Per serving 591 kcalories, protein 42g, carbohydrate 47g, fat 27g, saturated fat 16g, fibre 5g, sugar 9g, salt 1.97g

Make the most of quick-cooking ingredients and aromatic five-spice powder to create an appetizing and satisfying dish.

Chinese Egg-fried Rice

200g/8oz American long grain rice
cupful of frozen peas
2 tbsp sunflower oil
2 rashers back bacon, roughly chopped
1 small red pepper, seeded and roughly chopped
2 eggs, beaten
1 tsp Chinese five-spice powder
2 spring onions, shredded

Takes 30 minutes • Serves 4 (easily halved)

1 Bring a large pan of water to the boil, add one teaspoon of salt and then the rice. Stir once and return to the boil, then turn the heat down and boil steadily for 8 minutes. Tip in the peas, and boil for 2 minutes. Drain the rice and peas into a sieve and set aside.
2 Heat the oil in a wok and stir fry the bacon for 3–4 minutes until crisp. Add the red pepper and stir fry for a further 2 minutes.
3 Pour the eggs into the pan and stir fry until they are just set. Toss in the spice and the rice and peas, and stir fry until evenly mixed. Serve hot, topped with the spring onions.

• Per portion 344 kcalories, protein 12.1g, carbohydrate 48.9g, fat 12.4g, saturated fat 2.7g, fibre 2.5g, sugar 2.9g, salt 0.71g

For a nutritious and tasty meal, serve these stuffed baked potatoes with broccoli or another favourite green vegetable.

Shepherd's Pie Potatoes

2 tsp butter
½ onion, peeled and chopped
140g/5oz lean minced beef
250ml/9fl oz beef stock
1 tsp Worcestershire sauce
1 tbsp tomato purée
1 large jacket potato, baked
small handful of grated Cheddar
green veg, such as broccoli, to serve

Takes 50–60 minutes, plus baking time for potato • Serves 1 or 2

1 Melt half the butter in a non-stick pan and cook the onion for 3–4 minutes. Increase the heat and add the mince, then fry for a further 3–4 minutes until the beef has browned. Stir in the stock, Worcestershire sauce, tomato purée and seasoning, then bubble gently for 15–20 minutes until the mince is tender and the sauce has thickened.

2 While the mince is cooking, pre-heat the oven to 200°C/Gas 6/fan 180°C.

3 To assemble, cut the jacket potato in half lengthways and scoop the flesh into a small bowl, leaving the skin intact. Mash the potato with the remaining butter and season well. Divide the mince between the potato skins, then cover with the mash. Transfer the potatoes to a baking dish, sprinkle with cheese, and bake for 15–20 minutes or until golden.

• Per serving (if making for one) 779 kcalories, protein 50g, carbohydrate 79g, fat 31g, saturated fat 15g, fibre 7g, sugar 9g, salt 2.43g

The ultimate in comfort food – pasta and cauliflower
with a creamy cheese sauce.

Cauli Macaroni Cheese

300g/10oz tubed-shaped pasta,
such as, rigatoni, penne or
macaroni
1 small cauliflower, cut into florets
200g carton crème fraîche
2 tsp grainy or other mustard
175g/6oz Red Leicester,
grated
2 tomatoes, cut into wedges

Takes 30 minutes • Serves 4
(easily halved)

1 Bring a large pan of salted water to the boil. Add the pasta, stir well and bring back to the boil, then simmer for a couple of minutes. Tip in the cauliflower florets, bring back to the boil again and cook for a further 8–10 minutes until both pasta and cauliflower are tender but still firm to the bite. Drain well. Heat the grill to high.
2 Add the crème fraîche, mustard and all but a good handful of the cheese to the pasta pan. Stir over a low heat until the cheese starts to melt. Tip the pasta and cauliflower into the sauce and stir together gently. Season and transfer to a flameproof dish.
3 Scatter the tomatoes on top, then the rest of the cheese and a sprinkling of pepper. Grill for about 5 minutes until brown and bubbling.

• Per serving 636 kcalories, protein 25g, carbohydrate 64g, fat 33g, saturated fat 18g, fibre 5g, added sugar none, salt 0.98g

The easiest of dishes to make, using mainly storecupboard ingredients – perfect for those days when you're running low on fresh food.

Mixed Bean Goulash

2 tbsp olive oil, plus more for drizzling
1 large onion, peeled and finely chopped
1 tbsp smoked paprika
400g can chopped tomatoes with garlic
400g can mixed beans, drained and rinsed

TO SERVE
soured cream or natural yoghurt
toasted ciabatta slices

Takes 25 minutes • Serves 2 (easily halved or doubled)

1 Heat the oil in a large pan and fry the onion for 5 minutes until beginning to soften. Add the paprika and cook for a further minute, then stir in the tomatoes and half a can of water. Simmer gently for 10 minutes until thickened and glossy.
2 Tip in the beans and continue to cook for a further 2 minutes or until they are just heated through.
3 Spoon the goulash into bowls and serve with soured cream or yoghurt and toasted ciabatta slices drizzled with olive oil.

• Per serving 460 kcalories, protein 17g, carbohydrate 39g, fat 28g, saturated fat 11g, fibre 11g, sugar 15g, salt 1.68g

You can vary the topping according to what your kids like and, if you're short of time, use ready-made pizza bases.

Ham and Cheese Pizza

FOR THE DOUGH
500g/1lb 2oz strong white bread flour
1 tbsp olive oil
350ml/12fl oz water
7g sachet fast-action bread yeast
1 tsp salt

FOR THE TOMATO SAUCE
2 x 400g cans chopped tomatoes
½ x 200g tube tomato purée

FOR THE TOPPING
100g/4oz Cheddar, grated
100g/4oz cooked ham or bacon, cut into chunky strips

Takes 40–50 minutes, plus breadmaker time • Makes 4 (easily halved)

1 Make the dough in a breadmaker. To make the tomato sauce, mix the tomatoes and tomato purée in a pan. Bring to the boil, then cook for 10 minutes to boil off the liquid.
2 Pre-heat the oven to 220°C/Gas 7/fan 200°C. Divide the dough into four balls, dust with flour and roll out on a floured surface. If you sprinkle a little olive oil over the flour underneath the dough this will act as glue so you can roll the pizzas really thinly. Put the bases on to baking sheets and top with sauce, the cheese and ham or bacon.
3 Bake the pizzas for 15 minutes then remove them from the oven and take them off the baking sheets. Put them back in the oven, directly on the shelves, for a further 5 minutes.

• Per pizza 618 kcalories, protein 25.9g, carbohydrate 103.3g, fat 14.1g, saturated fat 6.3g, fibre 6.6g, sugar 9.6g, salt 4.17g

These roasted drumsticks can be cooked on the barbecue or under the grill if you prefer. The marinade also works well with fish and vegetables.

Sticky Chicken Drumsticks

4 tbsp sweet chilli sauce
1 tsp finely grated fresh root ginger
2 tsp soy sauce
finely grated zest 1 lime
8 chicken drumsticks

Takes 30 minutes, plus marinating
Serves 4 (easily halved)

1 Mix together the chilli sauce, ginger, soy sauce and lime zest. Pour over the drumsticks and leave to marinate for as long as you can (put them in the fridge if marinating for longer than 30 minutes).
2 Pre-heat the oven to 190°C/Gas 5/fan 170°C.
3 Place the drumsticks in a shallow roasting tin, shaking off and reserving any excess marinade. Roast for 20 minutes, then pour over the reserved marinade and cook for 5 minutes more or until sticky and browned.

• Per serving 200 kcalories, protein 26g, carbohydrate 4g, fat 9g, saturated fat 3g, fibre none, sugar 2g, salt 0.75g

This salad will keep in an airtight container in the fridge for up to two days. Stir in a couple of spoonfuls of boiling water before serving, as this will bring the salad up to room temperature and make it moist.

Tuna Pasta Salad

2 x 220g packs ready-cooked penne, or 200g/7oz dried penne
100g can tuna in oil
400g can beans (cannellini, borlotti or butterbeans are all good)
½ red onion, peeled and finely chopped
finely grated zest and juice 1 lemon
large handful of flatleaf parsley, roughly chopped

Takes 10 minutes • Serves 4 (easily halved)

1 Microwave the ready-cooked penne according to the packet instructions. If using dried penne, cook it in a large pan of salted boiling water for 8–10 minutes, or according to packet instructions, until tender. Drain well.
2 Tip the warm pasta into a bowl and mix in the remaining ingredients (the warm pasta will absorb the flavours). Taste for seasoning before serving.

• Per serving 238 kcalories, protein 19g, carbohydrate 31g, fat 5g, saturated fat 1g, fibre 5g, sugar 3g, salt 0.96g

Make this curry as mild or hot as you like and serve with basmati rice and warm chapatti or naan breads. If you keep any leftovers in the fridge and reheat the next day they will taste as good, if not better.

Sweet Potato and Pea Curry

3 tbsp curry paste
1 onion, peeled and finely chopped
2 large sweet potatoes (about 900g/2lb total weight), cut into chunks
450g/1lb potatoes, cut into chunks
600ml/1 pint vegetable stock
400ml can coconut milk
175g/6oz frozen peas
small handful of fresh coriander leaves, roughly chopped, to garnish
basmati rice, chapatti or naan bread, to serve

Takes 40 minutes • Serves 4 (easily halved)

1 Heat the curry paste in a large pan and stir in the onion. Cover and cook for 5 minutes, stirring occasionally, until softened. Add both types of potato, the stock and coconut milk, stir well to mix and bring to the boil.
2 Turn down the heat and simmer the curry for 20 minutes or until the potatoes have softened, stirring occasionally.
3 Stir in the peas, bring back to the boil and simmer for 2–3 minutes more. Taste the curry for seasoning, spoon into bowls and scatter over the coriander.

• Per serving 513 kcalories, protein 11g, carbohydrate 77g, fat 20g, saturated fat 14g, fibre 10g, added sugar none, salt 1.46g

Oats are a 'super grain' and make a perfect alternative to breadcrumbs here. The dried apricots and grated carrot give these low-fat burgers a sweet taste and prevent the meat drying out.

Turkey Burgers

2 tbsp olive oil
1 large onion, peeled and finely chopped
2 garlic cloves, peeled and crushed
85g/3oz porridge oats
450g/1lb minced turkey
100g/4oz dried apricots, finely chopped
1 large carrot, grated
1 egg, beaten

TO SERVE
8 bread rolls
cucumber slices
tomato chutney or ketchup

Takes 35–40 minutes, plus cooling
Makes 8

1 Heat one tablespoon of the oil in a pan and fry the onion gently for 5 minutes until soft. Add the garlic and cook for 1 minute. Add the oats and fry for 2 minutes more. Tip into a bowl and set aside to cool.
2 Add the rest of the ingredients to the cooled mixture with seasoning to taste. Mix well with your hands and shape into 8 patties.
3 Pre-heat the oven to 200°C/Gas 6/fan 180°C. Heat the remaining oil in a large, non-stick frying pan and sear the burgers on each side until well coloured (3–4 minutes). Transfer to a baking sheet and cook in the oven for 10–15 minutes. Serve in rolls with cucumber slices and chutney or ketchup.

• Per burger 179 kcalories, protein 16g, carbohydrate 17g, fat 6g, saturated fat 1g, fibre 2g, sugar 9g, salt 0.17g

These freeze well raw, if the fish hasn't been previously frozen. Freeze on the baking sheet until solid, then transfer to a rigid container and seal. Cook from frozen, increasing the cooking time by 5 minutes.

Curried Fish Fingers

3 slices bread (about 85g/3oz in total)
1 tbsp korma paste or other mild curry paste
4 thick white fish fillets (such as cod or haddock)
finely grated zest ½ lime or lemon

Takes 12 minutes • Makes 4 (easily halved)

1 Pre-heat the oven to 200°C/Gas 6/fan 180°C. Whiz the bread in a food processor until you have rough crumbs. Add the curry paste and whiz again until the crumbs are fairly fine and evenly coated in the paste.
2 Put the fish fillets on a baking sheet or tray and season on both sides. Sprinkle over the lime or lemon zest, then gently press the curry crumbs on top of the fish.
3 Bake for 7 minutes, or until the fish is cooked through and the topping is crisp and golden.

• Per fish finger 178 kcalories, protein 29g, carbohydrate 11g, fat 2g, saturated fat none, fibre none, sugar 1g, salt 0.64g

A basic tomato and onion sauce salsa makes an easy starting point for many pasta dishes. You could ring the changes and use bacon, salami, olives or capers instead of tuna.

Spaghetti with Tomato and Tuna Salsa

350g/12oz spaghetti
1 small red onion, peeled
500g/1lb 2oz ripe tomatoes
2 tbsp olive oil
pinch of dried crushed chillies
(optional)
140g can tuna in brine, drained

Takes 20–22 minutes • Serves 4
(easily halved)

1 Cook the spaghetti in a large pan of salted boiling water for 10–12 minutes, or according to the packet instructions, until tender.
2 Meanwhile, finely chop the onion and tomatoes and put in a large pan with the oil. Add the chillies (if using), and heat through gently for a few minutes, stirring well.
3 Drain the pasta and add to the sauce, then break up the tuna and add to the pan. Season if you like, toss well and serve.

• Per serving 367 kcalories, protein 17.4g, carbohydrate 23.3g, fat 23.4g, saturated fat 8.2g, fibre 4.5g, sugar 5.2g, salt 2.72g

This dish can be simplified by using baked beans instead of cannellini and omitting the treacle or syrup.

Flash in the Pan Bangers

1 tbsp vegetable oil
8 pork sausages
1 small onion, peeled and chopped
400g can cannellini beans, drained and rinsed
400g can chopped tomatoes
1 tbsp black treacle, or maple or golden syrup
2 tsp Worcestershire sauce or dash of Tabasco, to taste

Takes 40 minutes • Serves 4 (easily halved)

1 Heat the oil in a large frying pan until hot and fry the sausages over a medium heat for 20 minutes, turning them now and again, until deep golden and sticky. Remove the sausages from the pan and set aside.
2 Add the onion and cook for 3–4 minutes until softened. Tip in the beans and tomatoes, stir thoroughly and cook for 2–3 minutes, then stir in the treacle (if using), the Worcestershire sauce or Tabasco and 150ml/¼ pint hot water. Cook for a further 2 minutes or until slightly thickened.
3 Return the sausages to the pan and cook for a further minute or until bubbling.

• Per serving 367 kcalories, protein 17.4g, carbohydrate 23.3g, fat 23.4g, saturated fat 8.2g, fibre 4.5g, sugar 5.2g, salt 2.72g

These are a great freezer standby. Made in a large batch and frozen individually, they can be cooked to order when you want.

Crisp Chicken Bites

4 boneless skinless chicken breasts
6 tbsp red pesto
300g/10oz dried or fresh breadcrumbs
vegetable or olive oil, for greasing
tomato ketchup, to serve

Takes 20–25 minutes • Enough for 12 servings (easily halved)

1 Cut each chicken breast into 15 chunks, place in a bowl and mix in the pesto. Put the breadcrumbs in a large freezer bag, add the chicken chunks in batches and give the bag a good shake.

2 Spread out the coated chunks on a baking sheet lined with greaseproof paper, then freeze for 4 hours or until solid. Tip the frozen chunks into a freezer bag or rigid container, seal and freeze for up to 3 months.

3 To cook, pre-heat the oven to 220°C/Gas 7/fan 200°C. Pour a little oil on to a baking sheet – just enough to cover it. Put the baking sheet in the oven and let the oil get hot for 5 minutes. Tip as many frozen chunks as you need on to the baking sheet and bake for 10–15 minutes or until cooked through and crisp. Serve hot, with ketchup.

• Per serving 195 kcalories, protein 16g, carbohydrate 20g, fat 7g, saturated fat 2g, fibre 1g, sugar 1g, salt 0.65g

For a super-speedy midweek supper, this light and tasty omelette is the perfect solution – it's low in calories too!

Cheese and Tomato Frittata

4 eggs
1 tbsp Parmesan, grated
small handful of fresh basil leaves,
finely shredded
1 tbsp olive oil
50g/2oz soft goats' cheese, broken
into chunks
4 cherry tomatoes, halved

Takes 15 minutes • Serves 4
(easily halved)

1 Heat the grill to high. Crack the eggs then separate the yolks from the whites into two bowls. Tip the Parmesan and most of the basil into the yolks and season. Whisk the whites vigorously for about a minute until light and fluffy then, using the same whisk, beat the yolks with the Parmesan and basil. Finally, whisk the yolk mix into the whites.

2 Heat the oil in a small frying pan and tip in the egg mix. Leave to cook for a minute, then sprinkle the goats' cheese and tomatoes on top. Place the pan under the grill and cook for 5 minutes or until the omelette is puffed up and golden. The eggs should be set, with only the slightest wobble.

3 Scatter the remaining basil leaves over the omelette, then serve straight from the pan.

• Per serving 151 kcalories, protein 10g, carbohydrate 0.6g, fat 12.1g, saturated fat 3.8g, fibre 0.1g, sugar 0.5g, salt 0.41g

This is simple enough for kids to make themselves, then they can add as many extras as they like. The sauce freezes well, so why not make double and save some for a busy day?

Easy Cheesey Tomato Pasta

300g/10oz pasta twists (or your favourite shape)
1 tbsp olive oil
1 large onion, peeled and finely chopped
1 carrot, finely chopped
½ celery stick, finely chopped
2 tbsp leek, chopped
1 large garlic clove, peeled and finely chopped
2 x 400g cans chopped tomatoes
1 bay leaf
85g/3oz mild Cheddar, grated

OPTIONAL EXTRAS
2 tbsp sweetcorn kernels (canned or frozen)
1 tbsp frozen peas
½ red or orange pepper, seeded and finely chopped
2 tbsp mushrooms, finely chopped

Takes 40 minutes • Serves 4

1 Cook the pasta in a large pan of salted boiling water for 10–12 minutes, or according to the packet instructions, until tender.
2 Meanwhile, make the tomato sauce. Heat the oil in a pan and cook the chopped vegetables and garlic over a medium heat for about 5 minutes until soft. Add the tomatoes and the bay leaf, stir well and cook over a low heat for 10 minutes.
3 Drain the cooked pasta and add to the pan with your chosen extra ingredients. Stir well and heat everything through for 3–4 minutes. Taste for seasoning and serve hot, sprinkled with the grated cheese.

• Per serving 428 kcalories, protein 17.5g, carbohydrate 68.1g, fat 11.5g, saturated fat 5g, fibre 5.8g, sugar 10.5g, salt 0.82g

It's worth making up a large batch of marinade as it will keep in the fridge for up to two weeks and it can be used with chicken, steaks, sausages and burgers, as well as ribs. Great for summer barbecues.

Saucy Spare Ribs

12 pork spare ribs

FOR THE MARINADE
1 tbsp olive oil
1 onion, peeled and finely chopped
400g can chopped tomatoes
3 garlic cloves, peeled and finely chopped
85g/3oz muscovado sugar
3 tbsp malt vinegar
2 tbsp Worcestershire sauce
1 tbsp tomato purée

Takes about 2 hours, plus marinating
Serves 4 (easily halved)

1 Make the marinade. Heat oil in a pan and cook the onion over a gentle heat for 4–5 minutes until softened. Mix in the remaining ingredients. Bring to the boil and simmer for 30 minutes until thickened. Cool slightly, then whiz in a food processor until smooth.
2 Put the ribs in a large freezer bag and tip in about one-quarter of the marinade. Seal the bag and shake to coat the ribs in the sauce. Marinate in the fridge overnight.
3 Remove the bag from the fridge and pre-heat the oven to 200°C/Gas 6/fan 180°C. Tip the ribs and marinade into a large roasting tin and roast for 1 hour, turning the ribs over occasionally and adding more marinade if necessary. Reduce the oven temperature to 180°C/Gas 4/fan 160°C and roast for another 30 minutes or until browned and sticky.

• Per serving 341 kcalories, protein 21.9g, carbohydrate 28.9g, fat 16.2g, saturated fat 5.3g, fibre 1.7g, sugar 27.1g, salt 0.72g

A quick and effortless way of cooking white fish to create a crisp and light, low-fat dish.

Sesame Fish

100g/4oz breadcrumbs or 2 slices white bread blitzed into crumbs
1 tbsp sesame seeds
4 skinless white fish fillets (about 140g/5oz each)
2 tbsp natural yoghurt
1 tbsp olive oil

Takes 30 minutes • Serves 4

1 Pre-heat the oven to 220°C/Gas 7/fan 200°C.
2 Mix the breadcrumbs with half the sesame seeds. Brush the fish with yoghurt and coat in the crumb mix.
3 Lay the fish on a baking sheet and sprinkle over the remaining sesame seeds. Drizzle with a little olive oil and bake for 15–20 minutes.

• Per fillet 251 kcalories, protein 30g, carbohydrate 20g, fat 6g, saturated fat 1g, fibre 1g, sugar 1g, salt 0.71g

A wonderful winter-warmer for all the family. You can use reduced-fat sausages if you want to lower the fat content.

Sausage, Mushroom and Tomato Pasta

400g/14oz penne or other dried, short tubed-pasta shapes
1 tbsp sunflower or olive oil
454g pack good-quality sausages, cut into chunks
250g pack chestnut mushrooms, halved
500g pack cherry tomatoes
2 fresh rosemary sprigs, leaves roughly chopped
handful of flatleaf parsley, chopped

Takes 20 minutes • Serves 4 (easily halved)

1 Cook the pasta in a large pan of salted boiling water for 8–10 minutes, or according to the packet instructions, until tender.
2 Meanwhile, heat the oil in a deep frying pan and fry the sausages and mushrooms over a medium heat for 5 minutes or until the sausages are golden. Add the tomatoes and increase the heat to high. Cook for another 3 minutes or until the tomatoes pop and start to form a sauce. Add the herbs and seasoning to taste.
3 Drain the pasta and toss with the sauce.

• Per serving 681 kcalories, protein 29g, carbohydrate 86g, fat 27g, saturated fat 7g, fibre 5g, sugar 8g, salt 1.52g

This simple supper uses the microwave, so kids can help make their own 'pizzas'. Let them have fun changing the toppings to suit their tastes.

Potato Pizzas

4 small–medium baking potatoes, washed
200g can tuna in spring water, drained
½ x 170g jar mixed peppers, drained
2 spring onions, chopped
198g can sweetcorn, drained
200g/8oz Cheddar (as mature or mild as you like), grated

Takes 25–35 minutes • Serves 4 (easily halved)

1 Prick the potatoes several times. Arrange them so they are evenly spaced on a microwave dish lined with a double layer of kitchen paper. Cook in the microwave on High for 8 minutes. Turn them over and continue to cook for another 8 minutes.
2 Pre-heat the grill to high. Gently mix the tuna, peppers, spring onions and sweetcorn together with about one-third of the cheese. Season to taste with salt and pepper.
3 When the potatoes are cooked and cool enough to handle, cut them in half lengthways, leaving the two halves slightly attached. Open them out flat on a baking sheet, pile the tuna mixture on top and scatter over the remaining cheese. Grill for 5–6 minutes until the cheese has melted and started to brown. Pull apart to serve.

• Per potato pizza 385 kcalories, protein 24g, carbohydrate 29g, fat 20g, saturated fat 11g, fibre 2g, sugar 3g, salt 1.26g

Just five ingredients baked in a pan make an easy supper at the end of a busy day.

Oven Egg and Chips

450g/1lb floury potatoes, such as
King Edward or Maris Piper
2 garlic cloves, peeled and sliced
4 fresh rosemary sprigs or 1 tsp
dried rosemary
2 tbsp olive oil
2 eggs

Takes 1 hour • Serves 2

1 Pre-heat the oven to 220°C/Gas 7/fan 200°C. Cut the unpeeled potatoes into thick chips. Tip them into a roasting tin (non-stick is best) and scatter over the garlic. Strip the rosemary leaves from the sprigs and sprinkle them (or the dried rosemary) over the potatoes as well. Drizzle with oil, season well, then toss the chips to coat them in oil and flavourings.

2 Roast the chips for 35–40 minutes or until cooked and golden, shaking the tin halfway through.

3 Make two gaps in the chips and break an egg into each gap. Return to the oven for 3–5 minutes, or until the eggs are cooked to your liking.

• Per serving 348 kcalories, protein 11g, carbohydrate 40g, fat 17g, saturated fat 3g, fibre 3g, added sugar none, salt 0.22g

These tasty burgers are packed with healthy ingredients,
but they taste so good your kids will never know!

Veggie Burgers

2 tbsp olive oil
2 leeks, sliced
200g/8oz mushrooms, sliced
2 large carrots, peeled and coarsely grated
1 tbsp Moroccan seasoning
1 tbsp soy sauce
300g can red kidney or pinto beans, drained and rinsed
100g/4oz Cheddar, coarsely grated
200g/8oz (about 4 slices) granary bread, torn into pieces
burger buns, salad, tomatoes, ketchup and mayonnaise, to serve

Takes 30 minutes • Makes 8 (easily halved)

1 Heat one tablespoon of the oil in a shallow pan over a medium heat. Add the vegetables, seasoning and soy sauce, then cook, stirring occasionally, for 10 minutes until soft. Tip the contents of the pan into a food processor and add the beans, cheese, bread and seasoning. Pulse to a thick paste.
2 With wet hands, mould the mixture into eight burgers. These can be kept in the fridge for 2 days or frozen, stacked between greaseproof sheets, for up to 2 months.
3 To cook, heat the remaining oil in a frying pan and fry the burgers for 2–3 minutes on each side or until crisp. If cooking from frozen, allow at least an extra 5 minutes cooking time. Serve in toasted buns with salad, ketchup and mayo.

• Per serving 189 kcalories, protein 8.5g, carbohydrate 21.3g, fat 8.4g, saturated fat 3.3g, fibre 4.2g, sugar 5.3g, salt 1.44g

A satisfying supper from pot to plate in 15 minutes. Serve on its own, or with grilled tomatoes.

Cheese, Corn and Broccoli Pasta

100g/4oz farfalle or other dried short
pasta shapes
140g/5oz broccoli florets
198g can sweetcorn, drained and
rinsed
25g/1oz butter
100ml/3½fl oz milk
100g/4oz Cheddar, grated

Takes 15 minutes • Serves 2
(easily doubled)

1 Cook the pasta in a large pan of salted boiling water for 8–10 minutes, or according to the packet instructions, until tender. Add the broccoli and sweetcorn to the water for the last 4 minutes of the cooking time.
2 Meanwhile, melt the butter in a pan with the milk. Bring to the boil, remove from the heat and stir in the cheese until melted.
3 Drain the pasta and vegetables well, return to the pan and gently stir in the sauce. Toss to mix and season to taste before serving.

• Per serving 620 kcalories, protein 26g, carbohydrate 63g, fat 31g, saturated fat 18.2g, fibre 4.5g, sugar 6g, salt 1.75g

The sauce in this recipe is low in fat, made from storecupboard ingredients and totally hassle-free – just whiz the ingredients together and pop in the microwave.

Sweet-and-Sour Chicken

9 tbsp tomato ketchup
3 tbsp malt vinegar
4 tbsp dark muscovado sugar
2 garlic cloves, peeled and crushed
4 boneless, skinless chicken breasts, cut into chunks
1 small onion, peeled and roughly chopped
2 red peppers, seeded and cut into chunks
227g can pineapple pieces in juice, drained
100g/4oz sugar snap peas, roughly sliced
handful of salted roasted cashew nuts (optional)

Takes 20 minutes • Serves 4 (easily halved)

1 In a large microwave dish, mix the ketchup, vinegar, sugar and garlic thoroughly with the chicken, onion and peppers. Microwave, uncovered, on High for 8–10 minutes until the chicken is starting to cook and the sauce is sizzling.

2 Stir in the pineapple pieces and sugar snap peas and return to the microwave for another 3–5 minutes until the chicken is completely cooked.

3 Leave to stand for a few minutes, then stir in the cashews (if using) and serve.

• Per serving 305 kcalories, protein 36g, carbohydrate 38g, fat 2g, saturated fat none, fibre 2g, sugar 23g, salt 1.63g

If you prefer a veggie filling, omit the bacon and use 100g/4oz chopped mushrooms instead.

Sweet Potato Jackets

4 sweet potatoes
(about 300g/10oz each)
8 rashers bacon or 2 gammon steaks
2 tsp olive oil
1 bunch spring onions, chopped
200g can sweetcorn, drained
3 tbsp maple syrup or honey
1 tsp Dijon mustard

Takes 20 minutes • Makes 8
(easily halved)

1 Pierce the skin of the sweet potatoes with a fork, then microwave on High for 10–12 minutes until soft, turning them over halfway. (If you halve the recipe, reduce the cooking time to 6–8 minutes.) Halve the potatoes lengthways and scoop out one-third of the flesh from each half into a bowl. Place the potato skins on a baking sheet.
2 Heat the grill to high. Chop the bacon or gammon into chunky pieces, then fry in the oil for 5 minutes or until cooked. Add to the sweet potato flesh in the bowl, combine with the remaining ingredients and some seasoning, and mix well.
3 Spoon the filling into the potato halves, and grill until golden and heated through.

• Per ½ potato 477 kcalories, protein 15g, carbohydrate 83g, fat 12g, saturated fat 4g, fibre 8g, sugar 29g, salt 3.03g

With this Asian recipe, kids will love choosing what to eat with their child-friendly chopsticks.

Pick-and-mix Noodle Plate

2 boneless skinless chicken breasts,
or 200g/8oz trimmed pork fillet,
cut into finger-length strips
1 egg, beaten
50g/2oz breadcrumbs
200g/8oz medium egg noodles
2 tbsp olive oil
4 spring onions, chopped
½ cucumber
1 large carrot
hoisin, plum or barbecue sauce,
for dipping

Takes 35 minutes • Serves 4

1 Pre-heat the oven to 200°C/Gas 6/fan 180°C. Dip the chicken or pork strips into the beaten egg, drain off the excess, then roll in breadcrumbs to coat. Place on a non-stick baking sheet and bake for 15–20 minutes or until crisp and cooked through.

2 Meanwhile, cook the noodles according to the packet instructions. Drain and toss with the olive oil and spring onions. Using a vegetable peeler, shave the cucumber and the carrot into ribbons.

3 Pile the noodles on to serving plates along with the carrot and cucumber. Put a few chicken or pork strips alongside, and serve with a little pot of hoisin, plum or barbecue sauce for dipping.

• Per serving (without sauce) 388 kcalories, protein 24g, carbohydrate 50g, fat 12g, saturated fat 2g, fibre 3g, sugar 6g, salt 0.63g

These light and summery bowls are a good way to tempt the kids to eat lots of colourful fruit, and one cup provides two of their 5-a-day.

Melon, Orange and Raspberry Cups

500g box mixed melon pieces
(or chopped flesh from 1 medium melon)
finely grated zest and juice 1 orange
2 tbsp light muscovado sugar
150g punnet raspberries
ice cream or crème fraîche, to serve

Takes 5 minutes, plus 10 minutes standing • Serves 4

1 Tip the melon pieces into a large bowl, splash over the orange juice and zest and sprinkle with the sugar.
2 Mix well, then leave for 10 minutes or until the sugar melts.
3 Stir the raspberries through, then serve in small individual bowls or cups with a spoonful of ice cream or crème fraîche.

• Per serving 70 kcalories, protein 1g, carbohydrate 17g, fat 0.3g, saturated fat none, fibre 2g, sugar 17g, salt 0.05g

Making this is like performing a magic trick – just tip all the
ingredients into the food processor for instant ice cream.
The secret is to use frozen fruit.

Instant Ice Cream

250g/9oz frozen raspberries (or
other frozen soft berries)
2 tbsp golden caster sugar
squeeze of fresh lemon juice
250g tub Quark

Takes 5 minutes • Serves 4

1 Blend the fruit in a food processor with the
sugar and lemon juice until slushy.
2 Tip in the quark.
3 Blend well until it looks like ice cream and
serve immediately.

• Per serving 91 kcalories, protein 9.9g, carbohydrate
13.2g, fat 0.2g, saturated fat none, fibre 1.7g, sugar
13.2g, salt 0.10g

Give the family a fruity start to the day. This breakfast mix is soaked overnight so it's ready first thing – just pile some fresh blueberries on top before you serve it.

Overnight Muesli

250g/9oz porridge oats
100g/4oz sultanas
100g/4oz dried apricots, roughly chopped
50g/2oz hazelnuts, roughly chopped

TO SERVE
150ml/¼ pint unsweetened apple juice
2 tbsp natural yoghurt
fresh fruit, such as blueberries
2 tsp clear honey

Takes 10 minutes, plus overnight soaking • Serves 6

1 To make the muesli, combine the oats, sultanas, apricots and hazelnuts. Store in an airtight container.
2 To prepare for the following morning, weigh out an 85g/3oz serving per person and tip into a cereal bowl. Stir in the apple juice, cover and chill overnight.
3 In the morning, top with the natural yoghurt, fresh fruit and honey.

• Per serving 289 kcalories, protein 9.5g, carbohydrate 46.9g, fat 8.4g, saturated fat 1g, fibre 6.6g, sugar 19.1g, salt 0.04g

This pudding is fabulously fruity and delicious served with low-fat vanilla ice cream or natural yoghurt.

Juicy Lucy Pudding

350g pack frozen fruits of the forest, defrosted
3 tbsp light muscovado sugar
4 tbsp blueberry or blackcurrant jam
6 medium-sized ripe pears, peeled, quartered and cored
50g/2oz fresh white breadcrumbs
25g/1oz butter, melted
low-fat vanilla ice cream or yoghurt, to serve

Takes 45–55 minutes, plus defrosting time • Serves 4–6

1 Pre-heat the oven to 190°C/Gas 5/fan 170°C. Mix the fruits of the forest in a large bowl with the sugar and jam, then add the pears and toss to mix.
2 Tip into a deep baking dish measuring about 18x28cm/7x11in, cover with foil and roast in the oven for 20 minutes. Pierce a pear or two to see if they are really tender; if not, return the dish to the oven for another 5 minutes or until they feel soft.
3 Mix the breadcrumbs with the butter and scatter over the fruit. Bake uncovered for 10–15 minutes or until golden and crispy. Serve hot with vanilla ice cream or natural yoghurt.

• Per serving 281 kcalories, protein 3g, carbohydrate 58g, fat 5.7g, saturated fat 3.3g, fibre 6g, sugar 48.6g, salt 0.40g

A pud that's packed with fruit and so simple to prepare that young children can help make it – with a little guidance from an adult.

Quick Fruity Crumble

5 bananas, peeled and thickly sliced
350g/12oz frozen or fresh raspberries
250g/9oz digestive or gingernut biscuits
140g/5oz light muscovado sugar
¼ tsp ground cinnamon
140g/5oz butter, melted
ice cream or custard, to serve

Takes 30 minutes • Serves 6

1 Pre-heat the oven to 180°C/Gas 4/fan 160°C. Put the bananas then the raspberries into a 20cm/8in shallow, ovenproof dish.
2 Put the biscuits into a strong plastic bag and beat them with the end of a rolling pin to make fine crumbs. Stir in the sugar, cinnamon and butter so the crumbs are well coated. Scatter them evenly over the fruit.
3 Bake for 20–25 minutes until starting to colour. Remove and allow to stand for at least 10 minutes so the topping can crisp up. Serve with ice cream or custard.

• Per serving 551 kcalories, protein 4.5g, carbohydrate 74.7g, fat 28.1g, saturated fat 15.5g, fibre 3.4g, sugar 49.7g, salt 1.03g

This hearty, warming soup is full of veggie goodness
and boosts your 5-a-day.

Chunky Minestrone

3 large carrots, roughly chopped
1 large onion, peeled and roughly
chopped
4 celery sticks, roughly chopped
1 tbsp olive oil
1–2 garlic cloves, peeled and
crushed
2 large potatoes, peeled and cut into
small dice
2 tbsp tomato purée
2 litres/3½ pints vegetable stock
400g can chopped tomatoes
400g can cannellini or butter beans,
drained
140g/5oz spaghetti, snapped into
short lengths
½ small head Savoy cabbage,
shredded
crusty bread, to serve

Takes 40–45 minutes • Serves 4

1 In a food processor, whiz the carrots, onion and celery into small pieces. Heat the oil in a pan, add the processed vegetables, garlic and potatoes, then cook over a high heat for 5 minutes until softened.
2 Stir in the tomato purée, stock and tomatoes. Bring to the boil, then turn down the heat and simmer, covered, for 10 minutes.
3 Tip in the beans and pasta, then cook for a further 10 minutes, adding the cabbage for the final 2–3 minutes. Season to taste and serve with crusty bread.

• Per serving 420 kcalories, protein 18g, carbohydrate 79g, fat 6g, saturated fat 1g, fibre 16g, sugar 24g, salt 1.11g

A good source of vitamin C, this coleslaw is made partly with yoghurt, instead of all mayonnaise, to make it a healthier option.

Healthy Coleslaw

6 tbsp natural yoghurt
½ tsp Dijon mustard (optional)
2 tbsp mayonnaise
½ white cabbage
2 carrots
½ onion, peeled

Takes 10–15 minutes • Serves 6

1 Mix the yoghurt, mustard and mayonnaise together in a bowl.
2 Next, use a grater attachment on a food processor, or a box grater, to grate the cabbage and carrots. Either grate the onion or chop as finely as you can.
3 Tip all of the vegetables into the bowl and stir through the dressing. The coleslaw will keep in the fridge for up to 3 days.

• Per serving 76 kcalories, protein 2g, carbohydrate 8g, fat 4g, saturated fat 1g, fibre 2g, sugar 7g, salt 0.15g

Giving the kids all of their 5-a-day is easy with this veggie-packed supper.

Roasted Ratatouille Pasta

1 small aubergine, trimmed and cut into chunks
1 red pepper, halved, seeded and cut into chunks
1 courgette, trimmed and cut into chunks
1 red onion, peeled and thinly sliced
1–2 garlic cloves, peeled and finely chopped
1 tbsp olive oil
200g/8oz ripe tomatoes, chopped
175g/6oz penne
good handful of fresh basil leaves

Takes 45 minutes • Serves 2

1 Pre-heat the oven to 200°C/Gas 6/fan 180°C. Tip the prepared vegetables and garlic into a roasting tin. Drizzle over the oil, then season and toss together. Roast for 20 minutes, stir in the tomatoes and roast for a further 10 minutes.
2 Meanwhile, cook the pasta according to the packet instructions then drain, reserving four tablespoons of the cooking water.
3 Tip the pasta, reserved water and basil into the vegetables, toss and serve.

• Per serving 450 kcalories, protein 15g, carbohydrate 83g, fat 9g, saturated fat 1g, fibre 9g, sugar 16g, salt 0.07g

A superhealthy meal in a bowl – this satisfying soup includes three of your 5-a-day.

Hearty Winter Veg Soup

1 tbsp olive oil
1–2 garlic cloves, peeled and crushed
1 swede, peeled and cut into chunks
4 large carrots, peeled and cut into chunks
3 fresh thyme sprigs, leaves removed and roughly chopped
(or ¼ tsp dried)
850ml/1½ pints vegetable stock
500ml/18fl oz semi-skimmed milk
2 x 410g cans mixed beans in water, drained
crusty rolls, to serve

Takes about 25 minutes • Serves 4

1 Heat the oil in a large pan, then add the garlic and gently soften it without colouring it. Tip in the swede, carrots and two-thirds of the thyme, then pour in the stock and milk. Bring to the boil and simmer for 15 minutes.
2 Ladle a third of the soup into a blender, whiz until smooth, then pour back into the pan along with the beans.
3 Check for seasoning, then return to the heat and warm through. Serve sprinkled with the remaining thyme and some warm, crusty bread rolls.

• Per serving 307 kcalories, protein 17g, carbohydrate 47g, fat 7g, saturated fat 2g, fibre 14g, sugar 27g, salt 0.99g

A big, healthy sandwich packed with veg – this recipe will easily feed either one hungry child or two with smaller appetites.

Vegetarian Club Sandwich

3 slices granary bread
large handful of watercress, tough stems removed
1 carrot, peeled and coarsely grated
small squeeze fresh lemon juice
1 tbsp olive oil
2 dessertspoons reduced-fat houmous
1–2 tomatoes, thickly sliced

Takes 10 minutes • Makes 1 big sandwich

1 Toast the bread. Meanwhile, mix the watercress, carrot, lemon juice and olive oil together in a small bowl.
2 Spread the houmous over each slice of toast. Top one slice with half of the watercress and carrot salad and some tomato slices, then sandwich with another slice of toast and top with the remaining watercress and carrot salad and tomato.
3 Lay the final slice of bread, houmous-side down, on top of the tomato and press down. Eat as is or cut the sandwich into quarters.

• Per sandwich 299 kcalories, protein 11g, carbohydrate 50g, fat 7g, saturated fat 1g, fibre 7g, sugar 15g, salt 1.50g

For food safety, make sure that leftover rice isn't any more than a day old and that it has been chilled since it was cooked and cooled. Get it really piping hot when you use it to make your egg-fried rice.

Veggie Egg-fried Rice

1 tbsp sunflower or groundnut oil
1 tsp garlic purée
140g/5oz chopped fresh or frozen (thawed) peppers
handful of fresh or frozen broccoli florets, thawed
140g/5oz cooked rice, cooled
1 egg, beaten
light soy sauce, to serve

Takes 15 minutes, plus thawing time
Serves 2

1 Heat the oil in a wok or frying pan over a high heat. Add the garlic purée and stir briefly. Toss in the peppers and broccoli florets, stir fry for 3 minutes. Tip in the rice, then stir fry for another 3–4 minutes, so it's really hot.
2 Make a well in the centre of the rice and add the egg. Cook the egg, undisturbed, for 1 minute then stir into the rice.
3 Season to taste and spoon into serving bowls. Drizzle with soy sauce and serve.

• Per serving 218 kcalories, protein 6.8g, carbohydrate 25.9g, fat 10.3g, saturated fat 1.6g, fibre 1.6g, sugar 5g, salt 0.29g

This dish is a hearty and healthy way to use up any leftover cooked pasta.

Beany Pasta Pot

1 tbsp sunflower or vegetable oil
1 onion, peeled and finely chopped
1 large apple, cored and chopped
410g can chopped tomatoes (with garlic and herbs, optional)
300ml carton passata
290g can borlotti beans, drained and rinsed
3 tbsp red pesto
300g/10oz cooked pasta
crusty bread, to serve

Takes 20 minutes • Serves 4

1 Heat the oil in a pan and gently fry the onion for 3 minutes. Stir in the apple and cook for 2–3 minutes until both have softened. Stir in the tomatoes, passata and beans.
2 Bring to the boil, then simmer gently for 10 minutes.
3 Stir in the pesto and pasta, mixing well until the pasta is heated through. Serve in bowls with crusty bread.

• Per serving 233 kcalories, protein 10g, carbohydrate 35g, fat 7g, saturated fat 2g, fibre 5g, sugar 11g, salt 0.94g

A colourful mix of ingredients makes this an appealing quick lunch or supper for kids.

10-minute Tuna Bean Salad

1 carrot, peeled, coarsely grated
1 red pepper, seeded and sliced
100g pack sugar snap peas, finely sliced
410g can cannellini or butter beans, drained and rinsed
130g bag salad leaves
3 tbsp your family's favourite dressing, bought or home-made, plus extra for drizzling
200g can tuna in brine, drained

Takes 10 minutes • Serves 4

1 Mix the carrot, pepper, sugar snap peas and beans together in a large bowl.
2 Gently toss in the salad leaves and half of the dressing, then flake over the tuna.
3 Drizzle with more dressing as you serve the salad.

• Per serving 211 kcalories, protein 16g, carbohydrate 18g, fat 9g, saturated fat 1g, fibre 5g, added sugar none, salt 1.2g

This continental version of a favourite family supper – a classic cottage pie – is a sneaky way of getting children to eat more vegetables without realizing it.

Rösti Bolognese Pie

700g/1lb 9oz potatoes
4 medium carrots
2 celery sticks
1 garlic clove
2 tbsp olive oil
500g pack lean minced beef
400g can chopped tomatoes
350g jar sweet red pepper sauce
50g/2oz Cheddar, grated

Takes 1¼–1½ hours • Serves 4

1 Boil the potatoes for 15 minutes until tender. Drain, let cool. Chop the carrots, celery and garlic in a food processor. Heat half the oil in a pan with a lid and add the vegetables. Cover and cook over a medium heat for 5 minutes, stirring frequently.
2 Raise the heat to high, remove lid, and cook for 2 minutes. Add the beef and cook, stirring, for 3 minutes until browned. Add the tomatoes, pepper sauce and four tablespoons of water. Bring to the boil. Cover and simmer over a low heat for 25 minutes.
3 Pre-heat the oven to 200°C/Gas 6/fan 180°C. Peel the potatoes and grate into a bowl. Lightly mix in remaining oil and three-quarters of the cheese. Spoon the beef into an ovenproof dish. Cover with rösti topping, sprinkle with remaining cheese. Bake for 35 minutes until bubbling and golden.

• Per serving 573 kcalories, protein 37.7g, carbohydrate 46.5g, fat 27.5g, saturated fat 9.6, fibre 6.8g, sugar 16g, salt 1.73g

A great storecupboard stand-by that's brimming with easy-to-eat vegetables, pasta and beans – perfect for those days when your children bring home hungry friends for tea.

Storecupboard Minestrone Pasta

2 tbsp olive oil
1 small onion, peeled and finely chopped
2 tbsp tomato purée
300g/10oz frozen mixed vegetables (including peas, sweetcorn, carrots and broccoli – but not the chunky stewpacks)
700ml/1¼ pints hot vegetable stock
175g/6oz small pasta shapes, such as conchigliette
220g can baked beans
grated Cheddar, to serve

Takes 25–35 minutes • Serves 4

1 Heat the olive oil in a pan over a medium heat and gently fry the onion for few minutes until it starts to soften. Stir in the tomato purée, then tip in the frozen vegetables and pour in the stock.
2 Bring to the boil, add the pasta and stir. Cover and simmer for 12–14 minutes or until the pasta is cooked.
3 Stir in the beans and heat through, then taste for seasoning. Serve hot, with a bowl of grated Cheddar for sprinkling over the top.

• Per serving 294 kcalories, protein 11g, carbohydrate 49g, fat 7g, saturated fat 1g, fibre 4g, sugar 2g, salt 1.58g

Creamy tomato soup is the stuff of childhood, and this recipe is so simple you'll want to make your own for your children to enjoy its real flavour.

Real Tomato Soup

2 tbsp olive oil
1 onion, peeled and chopped
1 garlic clove, peeled and finely chopped
1 tbsp tomato purée
400g can chopped tomatoes
handful of fresh basil leaves, roughly torn
pinch of bicarbonate of soda
600ml/1pint milk

Takes 30 minutes • Serves 4

1 Heat the olive oil in a large pan, tip in the onion and garlic. Cook over a moderate heat for 5 minutes, until the onion has softened. Stir in the tomato purée, tip in the chopped tomatoes and basil leaves. Bring to the boil.

2 Turn the heat down, let it simmer for about 15 minutes until thick and full of flavour. For a smooth soup, whiz the mixture at this point to form a smooth sauce.

3 To finish the soup, tip the tomato mixture into a pan. Spoon the bicarbonate of soda (this stops the milk from curdling) into a small bowl and pour over one tablespoon or so of the milk. Mix until smooth, then tip into the tomato mix and pour in the milk. Bring the soup to a boil (the mixture will froth, but don't worry – it will go away). Gently simmer for about 5 minutes.

• Per serving 151 kcalories, protein 7g, carbohydrate 13g, fat 8g, saturated fat 2g, fibre 2g, sugar 11g, salt 0.51g

It can be hard to get children to eat enough fresh fruit and veg, but this risotto cleverly sneaks vitamins and fibre into their diet by using lots of veg.

Creamy Veggie Risotto

1 tbsp olive oil
1 onion, peeled and chopped
1 parsnip, peeled and finely diced
2 medium carrots, finely diced
350g/12oz risotto rice, such as arborio
1 bay leaf
1.2 litres/2 pints hot vegetable or chicken stock
140g/5oz frozen peas or petit pois
50g/2oz Parmesan, grated

Takes 40 minutes • Serves 4–5

1 Heat the oil in a large shallow pan. Tip in the onion, parsnip and carrots, cover and gently fry for 8 minutes until the onion is very soft.
2 Stir in the rice and bay leaf, gently fry for 2–3 minutes until the rice starts to turn see-through around the edges. Add 300ml/½ pint of stock and simmer over a low heat, stirring until it has all been absorbed. Continue adding the hot stock, sitrring in a ladleful at a time. Continue until the rice is just cooked and all the stock has been used. Add a little more water or stock if needed. This will take 18–20 minutes.
3 Remove the bay leaf from the risotto and stir in the peas. Heat through for a few minutes, add most of the Parmesan and season to taste. Serve sprinkled with the remaining Parmesan.

• Per serving for four 452 kcalories, protein 16g, carbohydrate 84g, fat 8g, saturated fat 3g, fibre 7g, sugar 9g, salt 1.28g

If you want some colour on this chocolate birthday cake, simply decorate it with candles. If you find piping the chocolate too fiddly, just drizzle it over instead.

Chocolate Birthday Cake

140g/5oz butter, softened, plus extra for the tin
175g/6oz golden caster sugar
2 eggs, beaten
200g/8oz self-raising wholemeal flour
50g/2oz cocoa powder
¼ tsp bicarbonate of soda
250ml/9fl oz natural yoghurt

TO DECORATE
1 tbsp butter, melted
2 tbsp boiling water
300g/10oz golden icing sugar, sieved
2 tbsp cocoa powder, sieved
50g/2oz each milk, plain and white chocolate, broken into squares

Takes 40–45 minutes • Cuts into 12 squares

1 Pre-heat the oven to 180°C/Gas 4/fan 160°C. Butter and line the base of an 18x28cm/7x11in cake tin. Beat the butter and sugar together until fluffy. Add the eggs beating well. Sieve the flour, cocoa and bicarbonate of soda into the mix. Stir in the yoghurt until smooth. Spoon into the tin. Bake for 20–25 minutes. Cool in tin for 5 minutes, turn out on to a wire rack to cool completely.

2 For the icing, pour the butter and two tablespoons of just boiled water into the sieved icing sugar and cocoa. Stir until smooth and spreadable. If it's too stiff, add a few more drops of water. Spread the icing over the top of the cake with a palette knife dipped in hot water.

3 Melt each chocolate in separate bowls. Pipe or drizzle 12 simple shapes over the top of the cake. Add candles and serve.

• Per square 432 kcalories, protein 6g, carbohydrate 65g, fat 18g, saturated fat 10g, fibre 3g, sugar 51g, salt 0.41g

Celebrate Mother's Day with these pretty cakes – they are so easy to decorate with ready-made writing icing and tiny sugar flowers.

Mother's Day Fairy Cakes

FOR THE CAKES
175g/6oz golden caster sugar
175g/6oz butter, softened
3 eggs, beaten
175g/6oz self-raising flour
1 tsp baking powder

FOR THE DECORATION
140g/5oz icing sugar, sifted
edible yellow food colouring
selection of writing icings (available in supermarkets)
ready-made sugar flowers (available in supermarkets from cake ingredients section)
20 paper cake cases

Takes 30 minutes, plus cooling • Makes 20 (you need 16 for decorating)

1 Pre-heat the oven to 190°C/Gas 5/fan 170°C. Put the cake cases into bun tins. In a bowl, mix together all the cake ingredients and beat with an electric whisk for 1–2 minutes, until evenly mixed.

2 Put a heaped tablespoon of mixture into each paper case. Bake for 15 minutes or until golden and well risen. Remove the cakes from the oven and cool on a wire rack.

3 Mix the icing sugar with four teaspoons of cold water to make a smooth paste, then colour with a drop or two of the yellow food colouring. Drop teaspoons of the icing on to each bun and spread to form a circle. Leave to set. Using the writing icing, pipe one letter of HAPPY MOTHER'S DAY on to each of the 16 cakes, using a sugar flower for the apostrophe and for decoration. Leave to set.

• Per cake 177 kcalories, protein 2g, carbohydrate 25.1g, fat 8.4g, saturated fat 4.8g, fibre 0.3g, sugar 18.4g, salt 0.33g

A childhood favourite that is enjoyed at any age – these dainty little cakes can be decorated for a young girl's birthday party, or for teenagers too.

Glamorous Fairy Cakes

FOR THE CAKES
140g/5oz butter, very well softened
140g/5oz golden caster sugar
3 medium eggs
100g/4oz self-raising flour
25g/1oz custard powder or cornflour

FOR DECORATING
600g/1lb 5oz icing sugar, sifted
6 tbsp water or half water and half fresh lemon juice, strained
edible green and pink food colourings
crystallized violets
crystallized roses or rose petals
edible wafer flowers

Takes 45–55 minutes • Makes 24 cakes

1 Pre-heat the oven to 190°C/Gas 5/fan 170°C. Arrange the paper cases in bun tins. Put all the cake ingredients in a large bowl and beat for about 2 minutes until smooth. Divide the mixture among the cases so they are half filled and bake for 12–15 minutes until risen and golden. Cool on a wire rack.
2 Mix the icing sugar and water until smooth. Use a third on eight of the cakes. Divide the rest of the icing mixture in two, then colour one half pale green and the other half pale pink and use it to ice the rest of the cakes.
3 Decorate the white-iced cakes with crystallized violets, the pink ones with the roses and the green ones with the wafer flowers. Leave to set. Will keep for up to 2–3 days when stored in an airtight container in a cool place.

• Per cake 193 kcalories, protein 2g, carbohydrate 36g, fat 6g, saturated fat 3g, fibre none, sugar 31g, salt 0.2g

A simple but stunning idea for a birthday cake, this recipe uses double the cake-mix quantity of the Glamorous Fairy Cakes (page 152). Decorate with your choice of colourful lollipops.

Lollipop Cake

2 x quantity cake mixture, Glamorous Fairy Cakes (page 152)
finely grated zest 2 lemons or oranges
about 6 tbsp thick lemon curd, plus extra for brushing
½ x 454g pack ready-to-roll icing
lollipops, candles, jelly sweets or Smarties, to decorate

Takes 1½ hours • Cuts into 12–16 slices

1 Pre-heat the oven to 160°C/Gas 3/fan 140°C. Butter and line the bottom of a 20cm/8in round cake tin. Make the cake mixture as explained on page 152, but adding the lemon or orange zest.
2 Bake for about 1 hour or until risen and springy to the touch. Leave the cake to cool briefly in the tin then turn out to cool on a wire rack.
3 To add the filling, cut the cake in half then sandwich it back together with the lemon curd. Brush the top of the cake with a little lemon curd. Roll out the icing and cut into a 20cm/8in round. Carefully put it on top of the cake, press down gently, smoothing it with your hands. Decorate with lollipops and candles and scatter over sweets.

• Per slice (when cut into sixteen) 353 kcalories, protein 4g, carbohydrate 49g, fat 17g, saturated fat 10g, fibre none, sugar 42g, salt 0.7g

A delicious, chocolatey Easter treat for the kids.

Chocolate Fudge Easter Cakes

FOR THE CAKES
140g/5oz butter, softened
140g/5oz golden caster sugar
3 medium eggs
100g/4oz self-raising flour
25g/1oz cocoa, sifted
16 gold cake cases

FOR THE FROSTING
85g/3oz milk chocolate, broken
in pieces
85g/3oz butter, softened
140g/5oz icing sugar, sifted
2 x 35g packs white-chocolate
Maltesers
mini foil-wrapped chocolate eggs

Takes 30 minutes • Makes 16

1 Pre-heat the oven to 190°C/Gas 5/fan 170°C. Put 16 gold cake cases into bun tins. Tip all the ingredients for the cake into a mixing bowl and beat for 2 minutes with an electric hand whisk until smooth.

2 Divide the cake mixture among the cases so that each one is two-thirds filled, then bake for 12–15 minutes until risen. Cool on a wire rack.

3 For the frosting, microwave the chocolate on High for 1 minute or in a bowl over gently simmering water. Cool slightly. Cream the butter and sugar together, then beat in the melted chocolate. Spread over the cakes and decorate with Maltesers and chocolate eggs.

• Per cake 274 kcalories, protein 3g, carbohydrate 31g, fat 16g, saturated fat 9g, fibre 1g, sugar 25g, salt 0.43g

A quick and easy decorating idea to liven up a
Christmas cake – or you could make it for a child who has
a December birthday.

Crayon Candle Cake

icing sugar, for rolling out
250g/9oz almond paste
1 rounded tbsp apricot jam, sieved
then mixed with 1–2 tsp water
20cm/8in round home-made or
bought fruit cake
1 egg white
200g/8oz icing sugar
5cm-/2in-wide strip white paper
5cm-/2in-wide strip greaseproof
paper, the same length as the
white paper
crayon candles
edible sugar stars

Takes about 30–40 minutes • Cuts into
12–16 slices

1 Lightly dust a work surface with icing
sugar. Roll out the almond paste on the work
surface to a 20cm/8in circle. Brush the top of
the cake with the sieved apricot jam, then lay
the almond paste on top to cover the cake.
2 Beat the egg white with a fork just to break
it up, then start to add the icing sugar a little
at a time, beating well, until you have a soft,
smooth, spreadable icing. Using a palette
knife, swirl the icing over the almond paste.
3 Decorate the strip of white paper with
Christmas drawings (the kids can have fun
creating their own design). Secure the paper
around the cake over a similar-sized strip of
greaseproof paper and secure the ends with
sellotape. Decorate the top of the cake with
crayon candles and sugar stars.

• Per slice (when cut into twelve) 444 kcalories, protein
5.2g, carbohydrate 79.9g, fat 13.7g, saturated fat
4.5g, fibre 0.4g, sugar 68.6g, salt 0.51g

This child-sized version of grown-up sandwiches will be a huge hit at children's parties.

Kid's Club Sandwiches

6 rashers smoked back bacon
9 slices square wholemeal bread
200g pack light soft cheese
1 carrot, grated
1 Little Gem lettuce (you'll need about 6 leaves)
12 cucumber slices (optional)
2 tomatoes, sliced

Takes 25 minutes • Makes 3 sandwiches

1 Heat the grill to medium high and grill the bacon for 5 minutes, turning once. Lightly toast the bread then cut off the crusts.
2 Mix the soft cheese with the grated carrot and spread over six slices of the toast. Top three of these with lettuce, cucumber and tomato slices, then a plain slice of toast.
3 Put two rashers of bacon on top of each stack, then top the sandwiches with the rest of the cheese-spread toast, cheesey-side down. Push a paper-topped (for safety) cocktail stick into each side of the sandwich, about 3cm/1¼in in from each corner. Cut each sandwich into four triangles. Keep together and wrap in cling film until just before serving.

• Per ¼ sandwich (triangle) 125 kcalories, protein 7g, carbohydrate 13g, fat 5g, saturated fat 2g, fibre 2g, sugar 3g, salt 1.10g

A fun version of traditional sausage rolls and ideal finger food for children's parties.

Sausage Roll Twists

½ x 500g block all-butter puff pastry, defrosted if frozen
400g pack pork chipolatas

FOR THE TOMATO DIP
6 tbsp reduced-sugar tomato ketchup
2 tsp malt vinegar
6 cherry tomatoes, finely chopped

Takes 30 minutes, plus any thawing time • Makes 24

1 Pre-heat the oven to 220°C/Gas 7/fan 200°C. Roll out the pastry to £1 coin thickness (about 20x30cm/8x12in) and cut into strips about 1cm/½in wide, cutting from the shorter edge.
2 Thin each sausage a little by twisting it, then snip in half. Wind one pastry strip around each half-sausage and place on a baking sheet, pastry join down.
3 Bake for 20 minutes until the sausages and pastry are golden. Meanwhile, mix together the ketchup, vinegar and cherry tomatoes. Serve in little bowls alongside the sausage twists.

• Per twist and dip 95 kcalories, protein 3g, carbohydrate 7g, fat 7g, saturated fat 2g, fibre none, sugar 1g, salt 0.54g

If your kids love pizza, they'll love this easy to eat version. They freeze well too if you want to prepare ahead.

Pizza Puff Pinwheels

375g pack ready-rolled puff pastry, thawed if frozen
6 tbsp ready-made pasta sauce (not too chunky)
100g/4oz wafer-thin ham
100g/4oz Cheddar, grated
1 egg, beaten
1 tsp dried oregano or mixed herbs

Takes 25–35 minutes • Makes 12

1 Pre-heat the oven to 200°C/Gas 6/fan 180°C. Unroll the pastry on to a lightly floured surface and roll it out to 40x33cm/16x13in. Spread a layer of pasta sauce over it, leaving a 1cm/½in border around the edges. Arrange the ham evenly on top then scatter the grated cheese over.
2 Starting at one of the short ends, roll the pastry up as tightly as possible. Chill in the fridge for 10 minutes or so.
3 Take a very sharp knife and cut the roll into twelve equal slices, laying them flat on two non-stick baking sheets as you go. Brush each pinwheel lightly with beaten egg and sprinkle over the herbs. Bake for 12–15 minutes until puffed and golden. Leave to stand for 5–10 minutes before serving.

• Per pinwheel 171 kcalories, protein 6g, carbohydrate 12g, fat 11g, saturated fat 5g, fibre none, added sugar none, salt 0.74g

Offer these around in individual pots to make sure that everyone gets their share of popcorn.

Sticky Popcorn Pots

250g/9oz popping corn
140g/5oz salted butter
140g/5oz light muscovado sugar

Takes 15–20 minutes • Serves 12

1 Put 50g/2oz of the popping corn in a lidded bowl and microwave on High for 2½–3 minutes. Tip into a big bowl and repeat four more times with 50g/2oz popping corn each time. (Can be made and kept in an airtight container up to a day ahead.)
2 Meanwhile, melt the butter in a pan then tip in the light muscovado sugar. Heat gently until the sugar has dissolved.
3 Pour the caramel over the popcorn and stir to coat. Cool, then serve in plastic cups.

• Per pot 192 kcalories, protein 2g, carbohydrate 25g, fat 10g, saturated fat 6g, fibre 1g, sugar 12g, salt 0.01g

Kids will enjoy tucking into these fruity pieces because they look really colourful and inviting laid out in rows on a flat plate.

Chocolate-dipped Fruits

100g/4oz good-quality plain chocolate, broken into pieces
10 clementine segments
10 pineapple chunks

Takes 10–15 minutes • Makes 20

1 Melt the chocolate in the microwave or in a bowl over gently simmering water. Dip the fruit into it to half cover each chunk.
2 Place the dipped fruit on a baking sheet lined with parchment paper to set.
3 Spear with cocktail sticks and lay the fruits on a large, flat plate. They can be made several hours ahead and kept in a cool place, loosely covered with cling film.

• Per fruit 32 kcalories, protein 0.4g, carbohydrate 3.2g, fat 2.0g, saturated fat 1.0g, fibre 0.4g, sugar 2.3g, salt none

A deliciously fruity party drink that's both pretty and fizzy.

Ice Cream Fizz

6 strawberries, sliced
12 scoops raspberry ice cream
or sorbet
300ml/½ pint sparkling elderflower
drink

Takes 5 minutes • Serves 6
(easily doubled)

1 Arrange the strawberry slices in the bottom of six pretty glasses (use plastic ones, for safety).

2 Top each with two scoops of raspberry ice cream or sorbet.

3 Pour over the elderflower drink and serve straight away.

• Per serving 234 kcalories, protein 4.3g, carbohydrate 34.8g, fat 9.6g, saturated fat 6.4g, fibre 0.1g, sugar 33.6g, salt 0.20g

This recipe is a twist on classic iced party rings, but the dough and icing work just as well when made into other shapes, such as stars or hearts.

Birthday Biscuits

250g/9oz plain flour
85g/3oz golden caster sugar
175g/6oz unsalted butter, at room
temperature, cubed
2 tbsp lemon curd
2 tbsp plus 2 tsp boiling water
250g/9oz icing sugar
1 tbsp strawberry jam

Takes 40 minutes • Makes 24

1 Pre-heat the oven to 180°C/Gas 4/fan 160°C. Whiz the flour, sugar and butter in a food processor to make crumbs. Pulse a little more to form a ball. Turn the dough out on to a sheet of lightly floured baking parchment. Roll out to the thickness of two £1 coins. Stamp out 24 rounds using a 5cm/2in fluted cutter and cut out the centres with the end of a piping nozzle. Lift the rounds on to baking sheets. Bake for 10 minutes until pale golden. Cool on a wire rack.

2 Mix the lemon curd with two tablespoons of boiling water until smooth. Sieve in 175g/6oz of icing sugar, stir until smooth. Mix the jam with two teaspoons of boiling water, sieve in remaining icing sugar.

3 Spoon lemon icing over the biscuits, then drizzle over the pink icing. Set for 20 minutes.

• Per biscuit 149 kcalories, protein 1g, carbohydrate 24g, fat 6g, saturated fat 4g, fibre none, sugar 16g, salt 0.01g

A soupy version of a classic chilli with a mellow taste so that children can enjoy it too. It's perfect for warming up a chilly Bonfire Night.

Chilli Con Carne Soup

1 small onion, peeled and finely chopped
2 garlic cloves, peeled and finely chopped
1 tbsp vegetable oil
500g/1lb 2oz lean minced beef
410g can pinto or red kidney beans, drained
2 x 400g cans chopped plum tomatoes
700ml/1¼ pints hot chicken stock
large pinch of crushed dried chillies
2 squares plain chocolate

TO SERVE
fresh coriander or parsley leaves, to garnish
Gruyère cheese, grated

Takes 1 hour 20 minutes–1½ hours •
Serves 6

1 Gently fry the onion and garlic in the oil for a couple of minutes until beginning to soften, then add the mince. Raise the heat and cook for 5 minutes, stirring from time to time, until the meat is no longer pink.
2 Stir in the beans, tomatoes, stock, chillies and chocolate and season with salt and pepper. Bring to the boil, cover and simmer very gently for 1 hour, or longer if you have the time. (You can make it up to a day ahead to this point, then cool and chill.)
3 Ladle into mugs or large cups and scatter with herbs, cheese and freshly ground black pepper. You'll need spoons to eat it.

• Per serving 252 kcalories, protein 24g, carbohydrate 14g, fat 12g, saturated fat 5g, fibre 4g, sugar 1g, salt 1.29g

These are great for dunking into a thick, hearty soup like the Chilli Con Carne on page 174.

Spiced Potato Wedges

1kg/2lb 4oz red-skinned potatoes, such as Desirée
25g/1oz butter, melted
1 tbsp tandoori curry powder or jerk seasoning

FOR THE DIP
1 tbsp Dijon mustard
1 tsp clear honey
5 tbsp mayonnaise

Takes about 40 minutes • Serves 6

1 Make the dip. Ripple the mustard and honey through the mayonnaise in a small bowl. Cover and chill.
2 Pre-heat the oven to 200°C/Gas 6/fan 180°C. Cut each potato into eight wedges, then cook in boiling salted water for 5 minutes.
3 In a large bowl, mix the butter and spice with a little seasoning. Drain the potatoes, then add to the bowl and shake. Transfer to two baking sheets and bake for 20–25 minutes, turning occasionally, until crisp and browned. Serve hot, with the dip.

• Per serving (potato wedges only) 162 kcalories, protein 4g, carbohydrate 29g, fat 4g, saturated fat 2g, fibre 3g, added sugar none, salt 0.14g

Bonfire Night wouldn't be complete without bangers.
Hand them out to guests as they wander outside to watch
the fireworks.

Hot Diggedy Dogs

2 tbsp sunflower oil
6 large pork sausages
1 large onion, peeled and sliced
1 tsp yellow mustard seeds
6 big flour tortillas
2 tbsp tomato relish
paper napkins, to serve

Takes 30–40 minutes • Makes 6

1 Pre-heat the oven to 200°C/Gas 6/fan 180°C. Pour the oil into a roasting tin and heat in the oven for a couple of minutes. Add the sausages and roast for 10 minutes.
2 Push the sausages to the outer edges of the tin and scatter the sliced onion in the centre. Sprinkle the onion slices with the mustard seeds, season and turn them to coat in the hot oil at the bottom of the tin. Return to the oven for 10–15 minutes until the onions are golden and the sausages are completely cooked.
3 Briefly heat the flour tortillas in the oven, a microwave or a dry frying pan, so they are softer and easier to roll. Place a sausage and some onion on each one, top with a spoonful of relish then roll, folding the bottom over. Serve wrapped in paper napkins.

• Per hot diggedy dog 351 kcalories, protein 11g, carbohydrate 37g, fat 19g, saturated fat 6g, fibre 2g, sugar 1g, salt 1.79g

There's no getting away from the fact that toasting marshmallows over the bonfire can be a bit messy – but they're all the better for it.

Chocolate Fondue and Toasted Marshmallows

400g/14oz plain chocolate, broken in pieces
85g/3oz unsalted butter
284ml carton double cream
300ml/½ pint milk
bag marshmallows, for dipping

Takes 10 minutes • Serves 8

1 Put the chocolate, butter, cream and milk into a pan, then heat gently, stirring occasionally, until the chocolate is melted and the sauce is smooth.
2 Thread the marshmallows on to long skewers, then carefully toast on the bonfire or leave cold.
3 Dip into the fondue and eat straight away. The fondue can be made up to a day ahead and reheated in the microwave for 1 minute on Medium, stirring halfway through.

• Per serving 609 kcalories, protein 5g, carbohydrate 55g, fat 42g, saturated fat 25g, fibre 1g, sugar 50g, salt 0.09g

A spooky idea for Hallowe'en muffins – perfect for hungry trick-or-treaters. Freeze them un-iced if you want to get ahead for a party.

Spider Web Chocolate Fudge Muffins

50g/2oz plain chocolate (55% cocoa solids is fine), broken into pieces
85g/3oz butter, cubed
1 tbsp milk, water or coffee
200g/8oz self-raising flour
½ tsp bicarbonate of soda
85g/3oz light muscovado sugar
50g/2oz golden caster sugar
1 egg
142ml carton soured cream
10 muffin cases

FOR THE TOPPING
100g/4oz plain chocolate, as above, broken into pieces and melted
100g/4oz white chocolate, broken into pieces and melted

Takes 40–50 minutes • Makes 10

1 Pre-heat the oven to 190°C/Gas 5/fan 170°C. Line a muffin tin with 10 muffin cases. Melt the chocolate, butter and liquid together. Stir and cool. Mix the flour, bicarbonate of soda and both sugars in a bowl.
2 Beat the egg in another bowl, stir in the soured cream. Stir into the flour mixture with the cooled chocolate, to combine. Spoon into the cases. Bake for 20 minutes until risen. Remove and cool.
3 Put two spoonfuls of melted plain chocolate into a small piping bag. Spread half the muffins with white chocolate from the bowl, allowing it to run. Pipe four concentric circles of plain chocolate on top of each. Drag a skewer through the circles at regular intervals, from the centre to edge, for a cobweb effect. Repeat, reversing the colours.

• Per muffin 349 kcalories, protein 5g, carbohydrate 45g, fat 18g, saturated fat 9g, fibre 1g, sugar 28g, salt 0.59g

The biscuits can be made a day or two ahead and then filled just before the trick-or-treaters start to arrive.

Orange Pumpkin-face Cookies

140g/5oz butter, softened
175g/6oz plain flour
50g/2oz icing sugar
finely grated zest 1 medium orange

FOR THE GLAZE
50g/2oz icing sugar
about 1 tbsp fresh orange juice

FOR THE FILLING
100g/4oz mascarpone cheese
1 tsp icing sugar
25g/1oz plain chocolate (55% cocoa solids is fine), melted

Takes 45–55 minutes, plus 1 hour chilling • Makes 12

1 Pre-heat the oven to 180°C/Gas 4/fan 160°C. Beat the butter smooth. Beat in flour, icing sugar and zest for a softish dough. Knead into a ball, wrap and chill for 1 hour.
2 Roll the dough out on a lightly floured surface, about 3mm/⅛in thickness. Cut 24 circles with a 7.5cm/3in plain cutter. Put the circles on baking sheets. Cut out Hallowe'en faces on half the circles. Gather up the spare dough, press into pumpkin stem shapes, trimming with a knife. Press on to the top of each face biscuit with a knife to join. Make pumpkin markings on the face biscuits. Bake for 15 minutes until pale golden. Cool.
3 Mix the glaze ingredients to a smooth, runny icing. Beat the mascarpone and icing sugar, stir in the cooled chocolate. Spread this filling over the plain biscuits and press the 'face' ones on top just before serving, otherwise they'll soften. Brush with the glaze.

• Per biscuit 219 kcalories, protein 2g, carbohydrate 22g, fat 14g, saturated fat 9g, fibre 1g, sugar 10g, salt 0.25g

Scary savouries for nibbling on at Hallowe'en. They are easy to make, so you can get the kids to help.

Garlic Eyeballs with Creamy Chive Dip

145g pack pizza dough mix
1 tbsp olive oil
flour, for kneading
1 large garlic clove, peeled and crushed
2 tbsp chopped fresh parsley
12 pitted black olives (optional)
1 egg, beaten

FOR THE DIP
142ml carton soured cream (or thick Greek yoghurt)
squeeze fresh lemon juice
2 tbsp snipped fresh chives, reserve some to garnish

Takes about 35 minutes, plus rising
Makes 12

1 Empty the dough into a bowl. Mix with water and olive oil, according to the packet instructions, so it's slightly sticky. Knead for 5 minutes on a floured surface until smooth. Lift into a large, lightly oiled bowl, cover with cling film and leave in a warm place until doubled in size, about 20 minutes. Pre-heat the oven to 200°C/Gas 6/fan 180°C.

2 Tip the dough on to the work surface, flatten, sprinkle over the garlic and parsley. Knead for 1 minute to distribute the garlic and parsley. Pull the dough into twelve walnut-sized pieces and roll into balls. If your kids like olives, poke one into each ball.

3 Brush each ball with beaten egg and bake on a baking sheet for 10–12 minutes until golden and risen. Meanwhile, mix together all the dip ingredients. Serve with the eyeballs.

• Per eyeball 81 kcalories, protein 2g, carbohydrate 9g, fat 4g, saturated fat 2g, fibre 1g, sugar 1g, salt 0.31g

Children will love these fruity pancakes – they're perfect
for Pancake Day – or any other day.

American Blueberry Pancakes

200g/8oz self-raising flour
1 tsp baking powder
1 egg
300ml/½ pint milk
knob of butter, melted
150g punnet blueberries
sunflower oil or a little butter,
for cooking
golden or maple syrup, to serve

Takes 25–35 minutes • Makes
10 pancakes

1 Mix the flour, baking powder and a pinch
of salt in a large bowl. Beat the egg with the
milk, make a well in the centre of the dry
ingredients and whisk in the milk to make a
thick, smooth batter. Beat in the melted butter
and gently stir in half the blueberries.
2 Heat a teaspoon of oil or knob of butter
in a large, non-stick frying pan. Drop a large
tablespoon of the batter, per pancake, into
the pan to make pancakes about 7.5cm/3in
across. Make three or four pancakes at
a time. Cook for about 3 minutes over a
medium heat until small bubbles appear on
the surface of each pancake, then turn and
cook for another 2–3 minutes until golden.
3 Cover with kitchen paper to keep warm
while you use up the rest of the batter. Serve
with syrup and the remaining blueberries.

• Per pancake (without syrup) 108 kcalories, protein
4g, carbohydrate 18g, fat 3g, saturated fat 1g, fibre 1g,
added sugar none, salt 0.41g

A healthy, low-fat pudding that takes only minutes to prepare.

Banana Yoghurt Pots

450g carton thick natural yoghurt
3–4 bananas, cut into chunks
4 tbsp dark muscovado sugar
25g/1oz walnuts, toasted and
chopped

Takes 5 minutes • Serves 4

1 Take four small glasses and dollop about one tablespoon of yoghurt into the bottom of each. Add a layer of banana, then some more yoghurt.
2 Repeat the layers until the glasses are full.
3 Scatter over the sugar and nuts, then leave in the fridge for 20 minutes until the sugar has dissolved.

• Per pot 230 kcalories, protein 7g, carbohydrate 40g, fat 6g, saturated fat 1g, fibre 1g, sugar 39g, salt 0.23g

To make as one big pie, put the fruit and sugar in a pie dish, lay the pastry on top, sprinkle with sugar, slash the top and bake for 30 minutes.

Blackberry and Apple Pasties

icing sugar, to dust
425g pack ready-rolled shortcrust
pastry
2 Bramley apples, peeled, cored
and chopped
2 tbsp light muscovado sugar
150g punnet blackberries
thick cream, to serve

Takes 35 minutes • Serves 4

1 Pre-heat the oven to 200°C/Gas 6/fan 180°C. Dust a work surface with icing sugar, then unroll the pastry and cut out four rounds using a small side plate as a template.
2 Combine the apples, sugar and blackberries and put a small pile on each pastry circle. Dampen the edge of the pastry then fold it over to encase the fruit.
3 Pinch and fold the pastry over, working along one edge, to make a pasty shape. Slash each pasty three times on the upper side with a small, sharp knife, lift on to a baking sheet and bake for 20 minutes or until puffed and golden. Serve warm, with cream.

• Per pasty 471 kcalories, protein 7g, carbohydrate 58g, fat 25g, saturated fat 10g, fibre 3g, sugar 20g, salt 0.85g

This crumble makes a quick weekday family-pud treat that needs barely any preparation.

Cookie Dough Crumble

500g bag mixed frozen fruit (whichever sort you prefer)
350g pot fresh cookie dough (such as Choc Chip Fresh Cookie dough)
cream, ice cream or custard, to serve

Takes 20 minutes • Serves 4

1 Pre-heat the oven to 220°C/Gas 7/fan 200°C. Tip the still frozen fruit into a shallow baking dish and scatter torn pieces of the cookie dough all over the top.
2 Bake for 20 minutes until crisp and golden.
3 Serve with cream, ice cream or custard.

• Per serving 457 kcalories, protein 8g, carbohydrate 57g, fat 24g, saturated fat 13g, fibre 6g, sugar 9g, salt 1.2g

An all-time children's favourite – you can reduce the calories by using low-fat yoghurt instead of ice cream, and if you like more crunch, top it with muesli.

Speedy Banana Splits

4 bananas
4 scoops vanilla ice cream
4 tbsp good-quality chocolate sauce
2 tbsp toasted flaked almonds

Takes 5 minutes • Serves 4

1 Peel and split the bananas in half lengthways.
2 Divide the eight halves among four plates.
3 Top with the scoops of ice cream, drizzle over the sauce and scatter with the almonds.

• Per banana split 418 kcalories, protein 8g, carbohydrate 61g, fat 17g, saturated fat 7g, fibre 2g, sugar 56g, salt 0.23g

You can't beat brownies, and these are perfect for tea after school or as a delicious pudding served warm with ice cream.

Best-ever Brownies

185g/6½oz plain chocolate, chopped
185g/6½oz unsalted butter, diced,
plus extra for greasing
3 eggs
275g/9½oz golden caster sugar
85g/3oz plain flour
40g/1½oz cocoa powder
50g/2oz white chocolate, chopped
50g/2oz milk chocolate, chopped

Takes 1 hour, plus cooling • Cuts into
32 triangles

1 Pre-heat the oven to 180°C/Gas 4/fan 160°C. Butter and base-line a 20cm/8in x 5cm/2in deep square tin.
2 Melt the chocolate with the butter. Cool. Whisk the eggs and sugar together in another bowl until thick and creamy and double their original volume. Pour over the cooled chocolate and fold together. Sift over the flour and cocoa and fold in. Stir in the chopped chocolate.
3 Pour into the tin, spread into the corners and bake for 25 minutes. If it wobbles in the middle, it's not quite done, so bake for another 5 minutes until the top has a shiny, papery crust and the sides begin to come away from the tin. Remove the brownie from the tin when completely cold. Cut into quarters, then into four squares, and finally into triangles.

• Per triangle 144 kcalories. protein 2g, carbohydrate 17g, fat 8g, saturated fat 5g, fibre 0.5g, sugar 14g, salt 0.06g

If you need an excuse to bake a cake for Hallowe'en, this is it: you can use leftover pumpkin to make this delicious treat.

Frosted Pumpkin Squares

FOR THE CAKE
300g/10oz self-raising flour
300g/10oz light muscovado sugar
3 tsp mixed spice
2 tsp bicarbonate of soda
175g/6oz sultanas
½ tsp salt
4 eggs, beaten
200g/8oz butter, melted and cooled slightly, plus extra for the tin
finely grated zest 1 orange and 1 tbsp juice
500g/1lb 2oz (peeled weight) pumpkin or butternut squash flesh, grated

FOR DRENCHING AND FROSTING
200g pack full fat soft cheese
85g/3oz butter, softened
100g/4oz icing sugar, sifted
finely grated zest 1 orange and juice of ½

Takes 50 minutes–1 hour • Cuts into 15 big squares

1 Pre-heat the oven to 180°C/Gas 4/fan 160°C. Butter and line a 30x20cm/12x8in baking tin. Mix the flour, sugar, spice, bicarbonate of soda, sultanas and salt into a large bowl. Beat the eggs into the melted butter, stir in the zest, juice and mix with the dry ingredients. Stir in the pumpkin. Pour the batter into the tin then bake for 25–35 minutes or until golden and springy to the touch. Check if it's done with a skewer.
2 For the frosting, beat the cheese, butter, icing sugar, orange zest and one teaspoon of the juice until smooth. Chill. When the cake is done, cool for 5 minutes then turn out on to a wire rack. Prick it all over with a skewer and drizzle with the remaining orange juice while still warm. Leave until cold.
3 Beat the frosting and spread over the cake. You can keep the cake, covered, for up to 3 days in the fridge.

• Per square 408 kcalories, protein 5g, carbohydrate 52g, fat 21g, saturated fat 13g, fibre 1g, sugar 37g, salt 1.33g

If your kids prefer other dried fruit to apricots and pears, simply substitute raisins, dried mango, cranberries, blueberries or papaya – in whatever combination they like.

Chunky Pear and Apricot Flappers

100g/4oz golden syrup
85g/3oz butter, cut into pieces
2 tbsp demerara sugar
1 tsp vanilla extract
140g/5oz porridge oats (use rolled organic oats if you can, as they have bigger flakes)
85g/3oz dried apricots, roughly chopped
50g/2oz dried pears, roughly chopped

Takes 35–45 minutes • Makes 12

1 Pre-heat the oven to 180°C/Gas 4/fan 160°C. Gently heat the syrup, butter and sugar until the butter melts, then stir in the vanilla, oats, apricots and pears until well combined.
2 Press the mixture into an 18cm/7in square, non-stick baking tin and bake for 25–30 minutes until golden.
3 Leave to cool for 10 minutes, then mark into 12 bars and leave to cool completely before removing.

• Per flapper 157 kcalories, protein 2g, carbohydrate 23g, fat 7g, saturated fat 4g, fibre 2g, sugar 11g, salt 0.17g

Index

213   Index

Picture and recipe credits

BBC Good Food Magazine and BBC Books would like to thank the following for providing photographs. While every effort has been made to trace and acknowledge all photographers, we should like to apologize should there be any errors or omissions.

Marie-Louise Avery p13, p15, p21, p73, p87, p149, p161, p163, p167, p173, p183, p185; Iain Bagwell p69, p117; Steve Baxter p41; Peter Cassidy p97, p115, p157, p197; Tim Evans-Cook p123; Ken Field p31, p45, p109; Will Heap p35, p71, p95, p103; William Lingwood p205; Jason Lowe p139; Gareth Morgans p11, p19, p33, p39, p59, p67, p77, p83, p85, p89, p91, p99, p111, p127, p129, p145, p171; David Munns p63, p93, p119, p169, p189, p201; Noel Murphy p187; Myles New p23, p65, p75, p125, p193; Lis Parsons p37, p57, p181; Craig Robertson p131; Roger Stowell p17, p61, p101, p121; Sam Stowell p43, p141, p143, p165; Martin Thompson p151, p159; Simon Walton p105, p133, p191; Philip Webb p153, p155, p195, p209, p211; Simon Wheeler p175, p177, p179, p199, p207; Jonathan Whittaker p107; Elizabeth Zeschin p25, p27, p29, p47, p49, p51, p53, p55, p79, p81, p113, p135, p137, p147, p203

All the recipes in this book have been created by the editorial team on *BBC Good Food Magazine* and regular contributors to the magazine.